morita therapy
and the true
nature of
anxiety-based
disorders
(shinkeishitsu)

Akihisa Kondo and Peg LeVine, Kondo's office, Tokyo, 1992.

morita therapy and the true nature of anxiety-based disorders *(shinkeishitsu)*

Shōma Morita

Translated by Akihisa Kondo

Edited by Peg LeVine

STATE UNIVERSITY OF NEW YORK PRESS

Published by
State University of New York Press, Albany

For information. address State University of New York Press,
90 State Street. Suite 700. Albany. NY 12207

Production by Marilyn P. Semerad
Marketing by Fran Keneston

Library of Congress Cataloging-in-Publication Data

Morita, Masatake, b. 1874.
    [Shinkeishitsu no hontai oyobi ryōhō. English]
    Morita therapy and the true nature of anxiety based disorders
(Shinkeishitsu) / by Shōma Morita ; translated by Akihisa Kondo ;
edited by Peg LeVine.
        p. cm.
    Includes bibliographical references and index.
    ISBN 0-7914-3765-5 (hc : alk. paper). — ISBN 0-7914-3766-3 (pb :
alk. paper)
    1. Morita psychotherapy. 2. Anxiety—Treatment. I. Kondo,
Akihisa. II. LeVine, Peg, 1952–   . III. Title.
RC489.M65M642713 1998
616.89'14—dc21   97-35187
                                                          CIP

10 9 8 7 6 5 4 3 2 1

contents

illustrations

translator's preface

This translation is made in commemoration of the seventieth anniversary of the founding of Morita therapy. *Shinkeishitsu no Hontai to Ryōhō* [True nature and treatment of anxiety-based disorders or *shinkeishitsu*] was authored by MORITA Shōma*, MD. and was published originally in 1928. It was then rendered into contemporary Japanese by KAWAI Hiroshi, MD. and published under the same title with Hakuyosha Press in 1960. This present translation is based on the original 1928 text.

Morita therapy was originally developed as a special treatment for clients with *shinkeishitsu* or those with anxiety disorders accompanied by hypochondriac thinking. Morita designed his treatment as a holistic and multifaceted therapy that progresses through four distinct yet related stages.

Although Morita wrote his book at the beginning of this century, his theories continue to provoke thoughts about the nature of psychotherapy and the nature of the human condition. Morita had great insight into the way the human mind interacts with the body. Also, he recognized the interaction between a person's health and her or his relationship with the natural world.

Although this four-stage treatment was developed in Japan and has its own cultural and language characteristics, it has been applied successfully in such countries as China and Australia. However, I have concerns about some possible

---

*The Japanese version of names is used throughout this text wherein the surname precedes the given name. The surname is put in capital letters at first reference only.

misunderstanding, misrepresentation, and misuse of Morita's theory and treatment by practitioners in some countries. If clinicians modify Morita therapy across different cultural contexts, careful consideration needs to be given to Morita's four-stage inpatient method. Hopefully, this translation will clarify and advance Morita's classical treatment.

More personally, I was trained in Morita therapy in Japan in the late 1940s. In the 1950s, I studied psychoanalysis with Karen Horney, MD., in New York. My forty-odd years of practicing psychoanalysis and supervision with Japanese and English-speaking clients has provided the foundation from which I translated this project. I have tried to select precise words from the English language to express various concepts unique to Morita therapy. This task has been the most trying part of the translation project. For example, Morita used Zen terms and other Japanese philosophical terms to express his basic ideas, but such terms are rather difficult to translate into English because of the contextual nature of their meaning. This translator fears that the reader might misunderstand the meaning behind some of Morita's terms. Therefore, I endorse the editor's footnotes and her glossary of Morita terms to assist the reader in grasping the context and spirit from which Morita wrote.

Because the original text was written in the late 1920s, the reader might find some of the diagnostic criteria to be odd or confusing. Therefore, the editor and I have assessed Morita's diagnostic criteria and applied the comparative diagnoses from the American Psychiatric Association's Diagnostic and Statistical Manual IV (DSM-IV, 1994).

As translator, I respectfully wish to acknowledge the following individuals. First, I wish to express my deepest gratitude to Dr. Peg LeVine for her most sincere contributions as chief editor; she refined my English and challenged the meaning of clinical and Zen terms so that they are realized in their original context by an English-speaking audience. I am thankful for her understanding and practice of Zen, and the way in which she wrote her Introduction and the Glossary of Morita Therapy Terms. My sincerest appreciation goes to the late Mr. HASEGAWA Yōzō; he gave me his kind and gentle encouragement to begin and to continue the translation of this book. I am grateful to Dr. Ishu Ishiyama (surname follows given name). He generously allowed me to consult his translation of Morita's work from Part Two (which contributed to the supplementary section in this translation); this appeared in the *International Bulletin of Morita Therapy* from 1988 to 1990. I also extend my deepest gratitude to Miss INOUE Akiko, and Ms. Gwen Burns, and Ms. Anne Boland who with tremendous patience assisted in administrative tasks. Appreciation is sent to Mr. OKAMOTO Tsuneo for his interest in this publication effort. I also wish to acknowledge the kind services offered by FUJITA Chihiro, MD., and KONDO Kyoichi, MD., in verifying the materials in the reference list. Finally, I wish to express my deepest appreciation to my wife, Toshiko, for her constant affection, encouragement, and support.

KONDO Akihisa
Tokyo, Japan (1997)

author's preface

The goal of medical science is to cure illness and enhance the quality of life. When separated from life as a whole, illness has no meaning. In these days (1920s), medical science is increasingly being divided into specialist areas; also, misleading advertisements about the benefits of lay medicine are rampant. As a result of these trends, both the therapist and client tend to focus on the disorder itself and ignore the whole person in her or his daily life. This situation is most disconcerting and can be depicted by the proverbs "Killing the ox by attempting to reshape the horns" or "Killing oneself by hanging, while taking an expensive herbal medicine."

One of my clients who suffered from a mild valvular disease of the heart had episodes of palpitation, dizziness, and other symptoms for more than four years. During these years, he searched for various treatments and rendered himself unable to work. I diagnosed *shinkeishitsu* (anxiety disorder with hypochondriasis) in this client and restored him to complete health through my special method of therapy. This client became much more active than before the onset of his illness. Yet, his physician was dissatisfied with the organic symptoms that persisted. Despite these symptoms, the client's distress disappeared and he felt healthy and active. The physician, however, took his client's change as a phenomenon that had nothing to do with medical treatment. This attitude seems to prevail among medical scientists today. Namely, they forget the total human being and focus narrowly on symptomatic changes alone.

Illness has both physical and psychological aspects. Most of the symptoms in the client described above were psychological and were not related to the valvular disease of the heart, the positive reaction to the Wassermann Test, or other findings. It is essential that physicians have knowledge about psychology and psychopathology in order to understand the meaning of mental symptoms. If a physician is ignorant of these fields, s/he is no better than someone who treats physical diseases without an understanding of physiology and pathology. It is regrettable when physicians limit themselves to the assessment of their clients' physical constitution without giving equal consideration to their psychological condition; also, I think the reality of clients' actual daily life requires assessment.

This small book was compiled from a series of articles written as a memorial to KURE Shūzō, MD. The articles have been corrected, supplemented, and rewritten in a comprehensible style. The purpose of publishing this separate volume in book form is to disseminate knowledge of the psychopathology of *shinkeishitsu*; I believe that symptoms of *shinkeishitsu* are present in most physical diseases. Simultaneously, I hope that further research in this field will be developed more vigorously by those who are stimulated by this book.

My study is not complete, of course, and my interpretations may be mistaken. However, I hope that other investigators will understand my intentions, discuss them, and exchange opinions.

MORITA Shōma
Tokyo, Japan (1928)

editor's introduction

Morita therapy was designed by the Japanese psychiatrist, MORITA Shōma (1874–1938). He believed that anxiety-based disorders share the same mind=body* interactions. In particular, he focused his work on the diagnosis and treatment of anxiety disorders, hypochondriasis, hysteria, and obsessive disorders.

Morita Therapy in Brief

In response to his clinical observations, Morita created a highly structured form of residential treatment. Essentially, his therapy is comprised of four consecutive phases that are designed to create paradoxes for the client to experience and endure.

Morita took clients into his home in order to create an environment of care, safety, and containment—particularly in the first two stages of treatment; he provided a therapeutic environment in a natural setting with outdoor work space for the successive periods of treatment.

Usually, each phase in the treatment has a duration of five to seven days. The sequence is as follows: (1) the initial stage consists of isolation and rest; it deprives the client of stimulation and requires her or him to remain in a confined room and to stay in a prone position; (2) the second stage consists of light, monotonous work that is conducted in

---

*From a Zen perspective, the true nature of body and mind is more accurately represented by body=mind or mind=body. In this way, dualistic assumptions about the suchness of the human organism are diminished.

silence. This stage facilitates boredom in the client so that s/he engages more fully in relationships with people, objects, and nature. In addition, the client's body rhythms find equilibrium. Journal writings often begin a written dialogue between the therapist and client at the end of this stage; (3) the third stage is comprised of vigorous, physical work that is performed out of doors; the client experiences her or his physical agility, weakness and strength. Additionally, art projects, such as pottery, wood carving, or painting are directed; spontaneity is enhanced; (4) and the fourth stage prompts clients to participate in purposeful activity with other people, while refraining from self-focused talk. Clients go outside the hospital premises for particular errands during this final period. It is essential that therapists assess clients for evidence of suicidal ideation, psychosis, intellectual disability, substance dependence, and violent behaviors prior to treatment as these are considered inappropriate for entrance into the isolation-rest stage. Also, the nature of traumatic history requires assessment.

The isolation-rest stage is very paradoxical and most essential to Morita's experiential therapy. In fact, Morita stated that, "It is the place from where my therapy begins." When a client enters the isolation stage, s/he is very "self" focused and absorbed in her or his own personal history and suffering; and s/he is very exhausted and detached from her or his body (such as sleeping, eating, and exercise rhythms are disrupted). Gradually, as the first stage progresses into the second stage, the client begins to engage her or himself in the environment; s/he attends to the changes in sunlight during the day, the sound of birds and insects, or textures of food. The more the client engages in "other," the more s/he notices a relief in her or his suffering. In the context of Morita therapy, "other" encompasses relationships to the whole ecological system, not just human relationships.*

During the course of treatment, clients tend to experience the fact that it is difficult to be anxious or depressed

---

*Following from Zen, the body=mind becomes the body=mind=environment.

while attending to life as that which falls outside the self. This fact is not described by the therapist to the client; rather, the experience of moving through the stages of therapy becomes the knowledge that informs the client. Also, the client may discover that her or his physical symptoms are a mirror to psychological symptoms. In essence, the experience of mind=body=environment becomes realized. Ultimately, Morita's treatment is designed to foster *akiraka ni miwakeru-koto* in the client ("clear discernment"), and *mushojū-shin* ("peripheral vision of consciousness") (see Editor's Glossary of Morita Terms).

Morita's Attention to Assessment and Diagnosis

Many people outside Japan do not realize that Morita was a contemporary of Sigmund Freud, William James, Henri Bergson, Mario Montessori, and Jean Charcot, to name a few. He reflected on the theories of his contemporaries and referenced them in his writing. Also, he was interested in treatment methods outside Japan, such as the rest therapy by Weir Mitchess, life normalization therapy by Otto Binswanger, persuasion therapy by Paul DuBois, and psychoanalysis by Sigmund Freud.

For instance, according to Morita, Freud referred to the "unconscious" as though it were a concrete structure located in the mind. In contrast, Morita contended that consciousness is transitory and is ever changing and flowing. And though there are similarities to William James's "stream of consciousness," Morita did not restrict consciousness to the mind. In this regard, he challenged Freud's later notion of ego (see "Ego or Ego-centered" in Glossary). Also, he used his particular understanding of consciousness and medical science to inform his diagnosis and treatment of clients.

In many ways, Morita was an early founder of cognitive, transpersonal, and experiential psychotherapies. In slight contrast to present-day methods, his treatment emphasized the importance of experiencing feelings (as a reality) rather than employing cognitive methods that are designed to shift or ignore feelings. For Morita, the cognitive shift in thinking occurs when the client does not interfere with feelings by mental manipulation or interpretation. Health is facilitated by therapeutic methods that return the body, mind, emotions, and consciousness to their natural flow. Ironically, if a client tries to 'endure' discomfort, s/he is disrupting the natural flow. This principle of emotions is very Zen-based. The client is most reliably informed by experience in this regard.

Additionally, Morita discussed the "storehouse of collected experiences" decades before Carl Jung contributed his theory of the "collective unconscious." Morita's theory of "consciousness," however, is much more mind=body integrated than Jung's theory. For instance, Morita discusses how experience is "embossed" into the body as consciousness experience (see section on Consciousness, Attention, and Association).

Regarding diagnosis, Morita stated that manic states and depressive states do not coexist as manic-depression. Rather one state flows from the other wherein a person with mania will move naturally into a state of melancholia after the mania passes. Morita referred to his particular understanding of consciousness when treating his clients. For example, when a person is left alone in an anxious state during the isolation-rest stage of Morita therapy, s/he notices the rise and fall of anxiety as a natural occurrence. Anxiety has a particular nature that cannot sustain itself at the same level over time; clients learn about the nature of their emotions during the course of Morita's four-stage treatment.

As a clinical contribution, Morita reclassified many of the psychiatric disorders that were used in Japan in the 1920s; though the Japanese system was similar to that used in the United States and Europe. For instance, the diagnosis of "neurasthenia" was prominent across countries at the turn of the century, but Morita challenged its criteria. He differentiated *shinkeishitsu* from other disorders. For example, those diagnosed with *shinkeishitsu* tend to be introverted in nature, whereas those diagnosed with hysteria tend to be extroverted (see "Extroversion" in Editor's Glossary of Morita terms). Assessment features of those with *shinkeishitsu* include: (1) a tendency to interpret certain natural emotions as negative emotions; (2) a tendency to exert intellectual control over one's emotional experiences, particularly with regard to uncomfortable feelings such as sadness, fear, and anger; (3) a tendency to deny the cycles and natural changes of human nature (physically, emotionally and psychologically); (4) a heightened awareness of and focus on one's self over other people and the environment; and (5) an exaggerated attentiveness to one's bodily sensations (or hypochondriacal tendencies).

Additionally, Morita coined the diagnostic category of "paroxysmal neurosis" and distinguished this disorder from general neurosis. Paroxysmal neurosis is very similar to the American Psychiatric Association's DSM-IV classification of Acute Stress Disorder (1994). Morita encouraged the differential diagnosis of hysteria, *shinkeishitsu*, and paroxysmal neurosis. Also, he encouraged clinicians to carefully discriminate between delusion that accompanies obsessive disorder and delusion that occurs at the onset of schizophrenia. Assessment is a critical phase of pretreatment and Morita postulated that those diagnosed with *shinkeishitsu* are more responsive to treatment than those with obsessive disorders and hysteria.

Morita contended that character disorders (classified as Personality Disorders in the DSM-IV) occur when a person becomes limited in her or his ability to adapt to change and responds to change with extreme sensitivity or dullness and distorted or faulty thinking. According to Morita, assessment of a client's character requires a clinician's attention to the context of the client's concrete daily life and a careful history of the onset of symptoms; he advises therapists to use both qualitative and quantitative measures for evaluation.

Morita recommended that careful assessment of the condition known as *seishin-kōgo-sayō* be given. This condition occurs when the client enters a vicious cycle of fixating her or his attention on symptoms. In essence, Morita designed his treatment to dismantle *seishin-kōgo-sayō*.

Zen Influences on Morita Therapy

The influences of Zen Buddhism, in particular, and Shintōism on Morita's theory and practice cannot be ignored. (Just as the influence of Christianity on the humanistic schools of psychotherapy in North America are apparent.) However, Morita did not want his method of treatment to be associated with Buddhism as a religion. Morita thought that his treatment would not be taken seriously as a reliable and valid therapy if people associated it with a religious or iconoclastic practice (personal conversation with KŌRA Takehisa, MD., Tokyo, Japan, 1992). Yet, his reference to Zen did not place him in a position of endorsing a religion because there is no transcendent God or god(s) in Zen that are the objects of the mind's focus; also, Zen is void of obligations or attachments to particular beliefs, ideas, and symbols. In essence, there is no separation between Zen and ordinary life. Likewise, because the Shintō perspective permeates all of Japanese society, people believe that there is no separation between nature and spirit—regardless of their religious affiliation.

According to Morita, Zen is not as simple as doing constructive activity (such that the third and forth stages of treatment alone are not progressive and full therapy and may, in fact, increase dysfunction). If constructive activity were presented as a central goal of treatment, then a person could become attached to activity—which runs counter to Zen.* Rather, Zen facilitates the development of one's peripheral vision of consciousness (*mushojū-shin*) or a "widening of awakeness" so that a person can respond to the uniqueness of each moment.

---

*There is an organization in the United States, "Constructive Living (CL)," which claims to adopt Morita therapy principles; however, CL does not attend to the fact that it is the nature of the evolution of the four successive stages that *is* Morita therapy. (The isolation-rest stage is crucial to taitoku or experiential embodied understanding).

In traditional Zen practice in Japan, methods of sitting have assisted the development of *mushojū-shin* (though the attainment of "clear discernment" is not the goal). Similarly, in Morita therapy, the peripheral vision of *mushojū-shin* just happens as the client begins the isolation-rest stage and moves through the successive stages of treatment; the "self" simply drops into the larger ecological system in which the person thrives. The client is no longer "self" focused and often experiences the self in ways that extend beyond "human"istic theories and practices. Of course, this is difficult to explain in words. (This Editor's Glossary of Morita Therapy Terms is offered to assist the understanding of subtle meanings in Morita's theory and practice).

It remains tricky territory today to decide when to point to the Zen principles that clearly run through the practice and theory of Morita therapy—and when to keep them hidden beneath clinical terms. In particular, because Japan is regarded as an "exotic" culture by many people outside Japan, Morita therapy is still at risk for not being considered as a practice grounded in clinical knowledge.

Future of Morita Therapy in English-Speaking Countries

Humans naturally classify and categorize time, people, places, events, plants, animals, diseases, and so on. Similarly, many theorists categorize the world of ideas and practices into "Eastern" and "Western." Unfortunately, this tendency to categorize has supported the belief that Morita's classical therapy cannot be applied in English-speaking countries because it originated as an "Eastern" method. (The isolation-rest stage is particularly controversial.)

And though differences clearly exist across countries, one cannot know what practices will or won't transfer across cultures until one attempts to apply them. (For example, though not originating in an English-speaking

country, many Non-Japanese people sit for long periods
of time in Zen centers in the United States, Canada, Great
Britain, and Australia.)* To date, many therapists in North
America have extracted some of Morita's theories and
methods (particularly from stages three and four) and have
applied them to outpatient counseling sessions without
first attempting to apply the therapy as Morita intended—
as a four-stage progressive treatment. I want to note that
the development of Morita-based counseling is well received in North America (particularly through the work of
Dr. Ishu Ishiyama). However, the understanding, ethics,
and advancement of Morita's "classical" therapy may be
in jeopardy if the four-stage treatment is not fully and
equally presented, applied, and researched.

Since 1992, I have been administering the classical residential Morita therapy in Melbourne, Australia to English-
speaking clients. (The first Australian case study was
presented at the International Congress of Morita Therapy
in 1993 in Fukuoka, Japan. The case was directly supervised
by Akihisa Kondo, MD.) I continue to follow the treatment
as originally designed and find that English-speaking clients
do complete the isolation-rest and successive phases in
much the same way clients report their experiences in
Japan.

The administration of Morita therapy in Australia has
been possible because Dr. Akihisa Kondo directly supervises
my work. He travels to Australia to collaborate in the clinical assessments, diagnoses, and treatment plans of my clients. Dr. Kondo's profound supervision has advanced the
reliability and ethics of Morita therapy in an English-
speaking country outside Japan. And though there are prac-

---

*As an historical note, in 1950 Karen Horney, MD. became interested in
the interface between Zen and psychoanalysis. She traveled to Japan in
1952 and spent time with D. T. SUZUKI, TAKEHISA Kora, MD., KONDO
Akihisa, MD., YOSHIYUKI Koga, MD., and staff at Jikei-Kai medical school
where MORITA Shoma, MD. had been chair. Unfortunately, Dr. Horney
died in 1952 and was unable to carry forward her observations and positive impressions regarding Morita therapy.

tical differences between clinical practices in North America and Australia (such as the influence of the managed-care health system on treatment in the United States), my practice in Australia demonstrates that English-speaking people do tolerate and benefit from the classical four-stage treatment of Morita therapy.

Editing Considerations

Morita's 1928 text is comprised of Part One and Part Two. The entire Part Two has become the main body of this translation project (with the addition of "Theories of the Unconscious" which was extracted from Part One).

The Supplementary Section (which was originally Part One) has been edited substantially in order to form a supporting section to the main body. The rationale for placing Part Two first has been: (1) to highlight that which holds relevance today for practitioners outside Japan; (2) to minimize the misrepresentation of and alterations to Morita's therapy by upstaging the holistic and progressive nature of his four-stage treatment; (3) to increase readers' awareness of Morita's attention to assessment and differential diagnosis; and (4) to invite readers to reflect on Morita's contemporaries (such as Freud) and how their respective theories of the unconscious affected their practices.

In my role as editor, and in collaboration with the translator, I deleted some of the case studies that were redundant. This translation has remained most literal across such areas as the development of *shinkeishitsu*, the four stages of treatment, the critiques by Morita of his contemporaries, and the Zen phrases. However, liberty has been taken to clarify passages in which Morita discussed differential diagnosis. In particular, psychiatric terms have been updated to coincide with those diagnostic categories of the DSM-IV. For example, Morita's term *obsessive ideations* has been replaced with *obsessive disorder*. Interestingly, Morita contended that an obsessive disorder is not directly related to a compulsive disorder as defined in the DSM-IV; he highlighted impulse control as a differentiating factor for assessment and treatment of these two disorders.

I have developed the Editor's Glossary of Morita Therapy Terms as a reference guide. In particular, language holds many meanings and the subtle distinctions of Morita's terms are essential to understanding his treatment. For instance, Morita uses the terms *emotional logic* or *emotional facts* to affirm emotions as holding significant emotional meaning; there is no need to interpret or evaluate emotions, to change them through intellectual manipulation, or to dismiss, ignore or deny their importance to action. Also, I have incorporated gender-inclusive language throughout the text and have chosen the word *client* in place of *patient*, and *therapist* in place of *psychiatrist*.

In Closing

My gratitude to Kondo sensei is felt beyond words. His commitment to and faith in the four-stage treatment of Morita therapy, his knowledge of English, North American and Australian culture, and systems of psychotherapy—as well as his commitment to the practice and spirit of Zen—have been of uncanny significance to this project. I think it is an honor to Morita Shōma, MD. that KONDO Akihisa, MD. has been the translator of this book.

I am particularly grateful for the on-going conversations I have had with WATANABE Naoki, MD. in Japan regarding the "meaning of bedrest"; he allowed me to interview one of his adolescent inpatients, and has been my most generous colleague during case consultations and Morita therapy conferences. Also, I appreciate the dedication by Dr. Ishu Ishiyama to Morita Therapy.

I am grateful for the heart-felt conversations with the late HASEGAWA Yōzō, and the late KŌRA Takehisa, MD. Also, I want to thank KONDO Toshiko for her creative spirit, and NETONAI Kachi for her nurturance and stamina.

Above all, I want to acknowledge Heather and Macahla for being so refreshing. And my warmest arigato to

Giovanni (for adventuring with me), Narda (for pushing and painting), Bill (for ironic laughings), Jon (for pulling it off), Tom (for brothering), Chris (for Kyūshū), James M. (for believing), J. Martin (for remembering), Scot, George, and Dorothy (for supporting), Walt (for the red Buddha), and Tippy (for sitting).

My work is dedicated to the late Stephen Welsh for the embodied memory of his "steam-roller" spirit; it's been a long run.

In closing, I want to offer the following passage from one of my client's journals during her experience in residential Morita therapy in Australia:

> The spider in the garden worked all night to build her web and the dog ran through it; the next morning the web was there again. She did not deliberate about how unfair life is, or what this disaster means, or who will comfort me—she just built her web. And when I saw the dew drops sitting on her web the next morning, that was all there was.

Peg LeVine
Melbourne, Australia (1997)

Figure 1. Shoma Morita, MD and his student and colleague Takehisa Kōra, MD (circa 1920s). (Photo: gift from the Archives of Dr. Takehisa Kōra)

author's introduction

The Treatment of Anxiety Disorders
(*Shinkeishitsu*)

The method of treating any illness is determined by assessment and diagnosis. It goes without saying that it is seriously unethical to conduct a treatment without being able to clarify the true nature of the illness and the pathology of the symptoms.

When making a diagnosis of *shinkeishitsu*, the clinician is asked to (1) exclude general organic illnesses, (2) differentiate the anxiety-based symptoms of *shinkeishitsu* from those of other mental disorders and personality disorders, and (3) explore any *shinkeishitsu* symptoms that are combined with other disorders, such as neurasthenia with exhaustion, and a predisposition to physical and mental hypersensitivity. Therefore, treatment requires a responsiveness to the context in which the illness occurs, the true nature of the symptoms, and the presenting condition of an illness; treatment is not to be restricted by a theoretical model. Additionally, therapists are cautioned against becoming too preoccupied with treating their clients' symptoms. Preoccupation with the treatment of symptoms is akin to "Killing the ox by attempting to reshape the horns."

In my view, the treatment of *shinkeishitsu* requires attention to the psychological makeup of the client. Further, the treatment requires a focus on realizing and strengthening those individual potentials that override the hypochondriac base, while breaking up and eliminating *seishin-kōgo-sayō*. *Seishin-kōgo-sayō* is the vicious cycle of the interaction between

1

one's felt sensation and one's focus of attention on the sensation; this is conventionally translated as "psychic interaction."

Given that the therapist's therapeutic purpose and means to attain the purpose can be contradictory or inconsistent, s/he is asked to specify an appropriate therapeutic method for each particular purpose. In order to clarify the major points of my therapeutic focus, I want to specify the psychological foundation of the present treatment, explain my special treatment methods, and further describe treatment for special types of *shinkeishitsu* (namely anxiety disorders, phobias, and obsessive disorders). Rather than discussing this further, I trust that the reader will know how to treat various anxiety-related symptoms and understand the strengths and shortcomings of various psychological and nonpsychological therapies.

1 principles of morita therapy

Shisō-no-mujun: Contradiction between Ideas and Reality

I coined the term *shisō-no-mujun* to define the opposing tension between one's desire that life and a sense of self be a certain way, and the facts about how life is and who one is. *Shisō-no-mujun* is directly translated as "the contradiction by ideas."

What I call "contradiction by ideas" results from one's attempt to create, manipulate, or modify facts by means of ideas, without knowing the difference between ideas and reality. Ideas are linguistic descriptions, explanations, or inferences of facts. Additionally, concepts are nothing but names or labels for things. They are like reflections on a mirror. Ideas and concepts are such reflections; they are not real entities or facts. That which is called *akuchi* (misplaced knowledge) in Zen, or *tendō-mōsō* (upside-down illusory thoughts) mentioned in the Prajuna Sutra, is manifest in the contradiction by ideas. For example, one could imagine possessing a divine power and flying in the air, and one could project such a thought into her or his dreams. However, it remains as imagination and is not a real fact.

Generally speaking, there are often contradictions and incompatibilities between one's subjectivity and objectivity,

3

between emotion and knowledge, and between intellectual understanding and experiential understanding. These contrasting elements are not identical. Contradiction by ideas occurs when one fails to acknowledge such distinctions. Therefore, when one moves away from contradiction and faulty thinking and returns to the true state of reality, one becomes free of contradiction by ideas and appreciates reality as it is. However, in the human process of intellectual development, a person often creates a wide gap between ideas and facts. The process is like making an error by one inch that results in a future difference of one thousand miles. Stimulus and reaction, and objectivity and subjectivity are accordant, much like sticking a needle into the skin and feeling pain, or catching a flu virus and feeling unusual about one's body. Similarly, there is little inconsistency between feeling affection toward one's own mother and the idea that one should love and respect her, and between understanding the distance between two objects and experiencing that distance.

However, when a person departs from one side of the fact and becomes progressively preoccupied with the other, s/he creates painful attachment to inner conflicts and repeats faulty thinking. Thus, as expressed in Zen, one creates "misplaced knowledge" and enters deeply into a state of confusion. I wonder if *satori* (enlightenment) means to break through such confusion and become one with the present reality, to go beyond verbal processing—where the external environment, the ego,* objectivity and subjectivity, and emotion and knowledge all become one and free of incongruities.

Subjectivity and Objectivity

Some clients complain of insomnia, heavy feelings in the head, dulled consciousness, and obsessional thinking. In

---

*The concept "ego" was translated into Japanese as *jiga* following Freud's introduction. However, Morita's reference to ego was Zen based. See "Ego or Ego-Centered" in *Editor's Glossary of Morita Terms* for clarification.

fact, these complaints are often reported by those diagnosed with *shinkeishitsu*. However, these are momentary feelings and they can vanish from a person's consciousness if s/he is unaware of such symptoms or if s/he simply acknowledges such symptoms in passing without dwelling on them. However, once a person focuses attention on a fleeting experience, a world of image is established and one becomes trapped in an illusory subjective world, independent of any objective stimuli that correspond to subjective feelings. In this instance, one's subjective experience is no less real than an objective one. Therefore, it is futile for a therapist to objectively manage and attempt to control their clients' minds by saying such phrases as, "Get hold of yourself," "Forget about the pain," or "Don't think of the symptoms." This kind of intervention is ineffective because clients are in a dreamlike state in which they cannot distinguish reality from nonreality; they believe the dream to be reality. I discuss the distinction between subjectivity and objectivity later in this text.

Emotion and Knowledge

A person's fear of death or fear of ghosts is a natural human response. The exaggeration of these fears is due to contradiction by ideas; it is useless to try to eliminate fears by intellectually saying to oneself that, "One can live one's life fully because of one's fear of death" or "Ghosts do not exist." According to "ordinary logic," one may objectively criticize emotional reactions by saying that there is no need to fear death. This is the reason I have discussed "emotional logic" and "emotional facts." The fear of death is a subjective fact in human emotional experiences. The descriptions and explanations of subjective and objective phenomena are referenced as "science." One's systematic and linear reasoning is called "logic," while one's unconditional obedience to absolute facts is called "faith." It is, therefore, faulty common sense to try to ignore or reject such emotional facts by intellectual means. I believe that one can make accurate clinical judgments by assessing emotional facts and by applying proper knowledge to them.

As an example of this relationship between emotion and knowledge, a person's feelings of discomfort and fear when facing a hairy caterpillar are emotional facts. While at the same time, the person knows that this insect will not spit poison or attack. A person who is governed by emotion would close her or his eyes and exit at the sight of a caterpillar. It is the intellect that guides the person to approach the insect and remove it. That is, one's ability to approach the caterpillar, in spite of the emotional discomfort as it factually exists, reflects the coexistence of emotion and knowledge. This is a reasonable response and a correct attitude, and it reflects an acceptance of the inner experience as it is, at that moment. On the other hand, it is the contradiction by ideas ridden with "faulty knowledge" that prompts one to first eliminate the uncomfortable feeling and produce a positive feeling in its place before approaching the caterpillar; this faulty process creates fertile conditions for the formation of an obsessive disorder.

Taitoku (Experiential Embodied Understanding) and *Rikai* (Intellectual Understanding)

Taitoku is the knowledge and awareness obtained from direct practice and experience, while *rikai* is abstract knowledge used to judge how things should or should not be and is based upon inference. Deepest understanding, therefore, arises after a person's concrete experiences bring realization in the body=mind. This can be compared to the fact that I cannot know how something tastes until after I have eaten it.

Personal interests and avocations are cultivated by repeated practice of corresponding behaviors. It is easy to understand with one's intellect about the sacred nature of work and to convince others of its importance. However, practicing what one advocates is quite difficult.

Shakamuni Buddha's great *satori*, attained after his six-year tribulation, can be condensed and understood as "impermanence," wherein nothing remains in the same state forever. This is manifested in the fact that all people eventually die; this is something that even a primary school child realizes. *Satori* involves the subjective experience of being one with the state of impermanence. This understanding is not theoretical. Following *satori*, intellectual understanding and experiential understanding become compatible with each other. And yet, when one is trapped in the contradiction by ideas and a state of confusion, there is an endless gap between intellectual and experiential embodied understanding.

Beliefs, Judgments, and Errors of Logic

Beliefs are formed as a person combines knowledge from her or his subjective, emotional, and experiential nature. A person translates experiential knowledge directly into actions that become expressions of her or his character. In contrast, intellectual knowledge and judgment influence one's behavior and character indirectly.

William James (1890) divides philosophy into the soft-minded and hard-minded schools. Thus, depending upon one's temperament, one's philosophy may have either an inclination to the subjective and mentalistic or the objective and materialistic. Therefore, the nature of one's attention, occupational interests, and judgment are influenced by one's psychological inclinations. On the one hand, the ways in which one develops personal ideas arise from one's temperament and belief system. When compared to beliefs that are acquired through experience, knowledge and ideas that are imposed arbitrarily are rarely effective or worthy.

The relationships between objectivity and subjectivity, and between knowledge and emotion require significant consideration in the treatment of *shinkeishitsu*. If a client's emotional base is ignored, any intellectual pursuit (by the therapist) only serves to increase the distance between the experiential mastery and therapeutic resolution. This inverse relationship is described by a Zen phrase, *keroketsu*, which is the state of a donkey tied to a post. That is, a donkey that is tied to a post by a rope will keep walking around the post in an attempt to free itself, only to become more immobilized and attached to the post. The same applies to people with obsessive thinking who become more trapped in their own sufferings when they try to escape from their fears and discomfort through various manipulative means. Instead, if they would persevere through the pain and treat it as something inevitable, they would not become trapped in this way; this would be similar to a donkey grazing freely around the post without getting bound to it.

Shinkeishitsu symptoms (such as a heaviness in the head or insomnia) result from a client's mental preoccupation with her or his own subjective experience. When such symptoms originate while one is in an emotional state, and one imposes logical evaluations to explain the symptoms, investigating the latter will never lead to reasonable solutions unless the fundamental subjective states are examined. This is similar to a common saying, "Affirmative and negative judgments made in a dream state are both unreliable." Taking a right-or-wrong judgment in the middle of mental confusion is also unreliable.

DuBois (1908) used his persuasion therapy for treating neuroses. He emphasized logical explanations and instructed clients to "totally eliminate the fear of illness" and to "become free from the past." It is likely we have all heard such comments from time to time and such advice appears within the realm of perfect common sense. Nonetheless, this approach ignores the reality of human emotionality. This belief is the same as convincing someone to love a caterpillar or to taste unpleasant medicine as something delicious. Furthermore, the psychological process of developing obsessions is linked to this type of mistaken logical thinking. For example, when a person thinks about uncleanness or facial flushing incessantly and attempts to suppress or manipulate her or his feelings through ordinary logic, s/he increases suffering. This approach-avoidance thinking only leads to more minute inquiry with one's mind and recovery becomes futile. An obsession originates from faulty judgments. If there were no flawed judgments, then this type of suffering from complicated ideational conflicts would not start in the first place. This is the reason that young children and those with intellectual disabilities rarely develop obsessive disorders.

Theories of the Unconscious*

Those who observe another person's death from heart disease, nurse a hemiplegic parent for a long time, or look at the body of someone drowned from a love suicide may later develop symptoms of anxiety in response to their experiences. Many investigators, including Freud and DuBois, have attributed neurosis to the unconscious or subconscious influences on the mind. However, neither of these investigators explain how certain emotional experiences enter the unconscious.

From my perspective, the mind does not stay still for one moment. The mind is always active and in flux. Zen proposes that, "Our mind changes according to various circumstances and the very point of change is very subtle. When one realizes her or his true nature according to the flow of the stream of mind, one transcends the world of emotional vicissitude." (See calligraphy by Shōma Morita, MD. on the following page.) In studying the mind, therefore, it is necessary to consider its dynamic flow and change between external events and the self. Freud and other investi-

---

*This section on the "Theories of the Unconscious" has been extracted from Part One of Morita's original text. Morita's use of the term *unconscious* is different from the meaning given by Freud. According to Morita, the unconscious is actually a phenomenon of consciousness that has a natural dynamic flow; disorder occurs in the mind when the natural flow is disrupted.

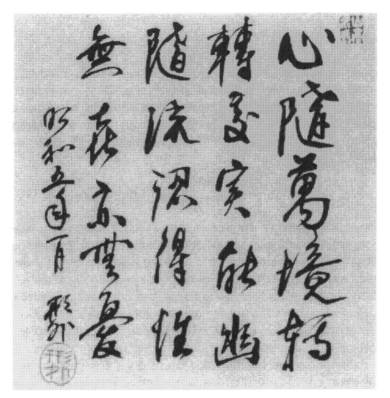

Figure 2. Calligraphy of Zen saying rendered by Shōma Morita, MD., signed as *Keigai* (circa 1920s).

gators have divided consciousness into concrete and separate parts that are personified and housed in the mind. I do not share this view. We have a song in Zen that goes as follows: "I wonder if the bell itself tolls or if the stick that rings the bell creates its sound. No, the sound arises from the space between the bell and the stick." This is analogous to saying that mental activity develops when the mind is stimulated by external events. Further, the mind is not located between the bell and the stick. No real or fixed body of "the mind" exists. Just as burning wood cannot maintain a constant form, so the mind is always active and changing; it moves between internal and external events. The mind is neither wood nor oxygen; it is the phenomenon of combustion. When the stick strikes the bell as an external event, the bell vibrates as an internal event, and an entirely new psychological phenomenon occurs. It is not true that the space between the bell and the stick strikes the bell. Likewise, it is not true that disorder develops because a specific active entity called the unconscious or subconscious is present.

"Complex," as described by Freud (1915) and other theorists, refers to a collection of images and ideas that cluster around particular experiences that carry strong emotions in a person. The agony a person feels after experiencing trauma (such as a severe heart attack or a major earthquake) is impressed deeply within the person's mind=body and may eventually become a source of anxiety. Thereafter, events such as an illness, an accident, family problems, or an episode of bad luck may be associated with a past experience (through association of ideas) and evoke the unpleasant memories regardless of the person's state of consciousness. The previous emotion becomes regenerated, reformulated, and exaggerated and forms the so-called complex (or constellation of associations).

Consider an experience I had seven years ago when my child suffered from pertussis at the age of four. Years later, a child in our neighborhood had the same illness and I could hear the child's fits of coughing. Whenever I heard this neighbor's child coughing, the previous emotion associated with my own child's illness flashed through my mind like lightning. I became concerned about my child and felt compelled to check his well being. When I told my wife about my response, she reported the same experience. The same emotion reappeared in me after many years. This illustration shows how adequate conditions and associations can stimulate a recurrence of a previous emotion.

The development of a complex is a common psychological process that can occur in many situations. Anxiety disorders occur when a person has a tendency toward hypochondriasis, which is not related to the presence of a complex. For example, individuals with hypochondriac tendencies may develop palpitations because of the anxiety or fear they experience when observing the agony in a person with severe heart disease. When the person later encounters similar conditions associated with the past experience, s/he may develop a panic attack instantly via the process of *seishin-kōgo-sayō*. However, if the person's hypochondriac tendency is very mild, *seishin-kōgo-sayō* will not occur even if a so-called unconscious movement is present; the fear will be experienced merely as a simple fear, without developing into symptoms of anxiety.

According to Freud (1916, 1917), psychoanalysis enables the person to pursue a complex and unravel it, or to uncover the cause of her or his anxiety or the past experience associated with the emotion. Thus, Freud assumed that the client could be healed or cured by uncovering and verbally and emotionally expressing any previous experiences associated with the emotions, or by understanding the relationship between the past experience and the present disorder. However, I think that Freud's practice is similar to the religious practice of confession and falls within the range of nosotropic therapy.

From my viewpoint, the treatment of anxiety-based disorders does not require the time or energy needed to uncover a particular cause, regardless of whether the anxiety originates at the moment a client witnesses or experiences a trauma. Essentially, I think it is sufficient to either eliminate the fear associated with *seishin-kōgo-sayō*, or to make an appropriate balance between fear and *seishin-kōgo-sayō*.

Nature and Artificiality

People tend to create various contradictions by ideas because of their confusion surrounding the relationships between such things as nature and artificiality, purposes and means, and results and conditions. Physical, emotional, and psychological activities of the human being are natural phenomena and cannot be artificially manipulated. However, people tend to believe that they can freely control these activities by will and by ordinary thinking. This is particularly true with regard to the psychological realm. For instance, most people know that they cannot physically lift their bodies in the air at will. When it comes to psychological matters, however, they believe erroneously that other people do not understand their mind, and they dogmatically think that they can freely do whatever they desire. Realistically, however, what one does is limited by the focus of consciousness on accomplishing an objective. The true nature of consciousness is to focus on the object and not the means to attain control of the object.

Mental activity is controlled by one's volition only when ideas are working toward a purposeful goal. Usually, however, ideas occur at random. Our sensations and moods, the sudden formation of ideas and dreams, and the human tendency to forget are definitely natural phenomena governed by the law of causality. They cannot be manipulated or managed at will.

Freud (1915) states that "forgetting" is caused by a psychological mechanism of repression due to an unconscious process. By looking only at the result, Freud regarded forgetting as a repressive mechanism. However, if this term is not interpreted as an unconscious process and is regarded as a person's conscious attempt to reject a certain thought, then unpleasant emotions enter awareness, get stuck in the foreground of awareness and become more difficult to forget. In this regard, forgetting is a natural phenomenon whereby certain thoughts become discharged from the incessantly flowing consciousness stream and become unavailable to conscious association and recall. A person cannot deliberately forget. Forgetting occurs in a split second. Not being able to understand when and how one forgets is comparable to not being able to remember when and how one falls asleep. Therefore, if one tries to forget something, to fall asleep in a hurry, or to suppress psychological activities, such attempts increase psychological conflict and disrupt the flow of consciousness. Ideational conflict results in consequences that run counter to one's intended purposes and the natural flow of consciousness. Such a phenomenon clearly illustrates nothing but the contradiction by ideas between nature and artificiality, and between purposes and means.

DuBois (1908) instructed his clients with such phrases as, "Be brave," and "Have confidence in yourself." There are comparable Japanese common sayings like, "Be determined in your death." "Be absolutely committed to the present moment." "Become free from intentions and ideas." These are all intended to motivate the achievement of certain purposes and results. What is meant by these sayings is that it would be desirable to attain such mental states. If, however, no effective methods and conditions are developed to help a person accomplish such states, then s/he will only become tired of futile attempts encouraged by these sayings; in essence, s/he ends up with unnecessary fatigue and opposite results. Responding to such encouragement is like riding a horse against a wall while hurrying in vain to a destination, or trying to wrestle with *noren* (a cloth curtain that is placed at the entrance of Japanese restaurants and shops). Paradoxically, attempts to induce a brave feeling create more timidity, and attempts to become unconcerned about death make people even more governed by their fear of death. True courage occurs when one is not aware of her or his own braveness. A true and resolute state of mind in response to imminent death is achieved only when one is not formulating ideas about death. Similarly, when a person tries anxiously to develop a strong religious faith, s/he moves farther away from one. One tells lies when forcing a confession, and one becomes impolite by trying to be perfectly polite.

The experiences of mindlessness, absolute commitment that extends beyond life or death, and enlightenment become images of the mind when one strives to attain them. Like an image reflected on a mirror, one becomes an object that is projected externally for observation, and therefore one is not "self" as s/he is. When people are fully mindless, absolutely committed, and become one with the present moment, they can no longer be aware of their own states. This is akin to the fact that one can neither see her or his own face directly, nor observe the whole image of a mountain when once s/he enters into it. The reason that people do not understand such a distinction is because contradiction by ideas governs their minds and confuses their abilities to distinguish between subjectivity and objectivity, purpose and means, and results and conditions.

Objective Projection of Ideas

One cannot generate courageous and self-confident feelings by will. Likewise, pain and suffering cannot be manipulated by one's desire to be free from them.

There are two ways of freeing oneself from uncomfortable feelings. One way is to completely become the pain or the suffering itself. When one is in a purely subjective state, one is entirely beyond evaluations due to dualistic or "subject versus object" ways of thinking. This is similar to one's inability to see her or his own face. This attained state is discussed in the section, *Obedience to Nature*.

The other way to free oneself from uncomfortable feelings is to focus attention on the pain, and to observe, describe, and evaluate it, without attempting to eliminate the discomfort or to distract oneself. In this way, the pain and suffering become liberated from being the object of subjective attachment; they become objective entities projected onto the external world. The attainment of this freedom is comparable to seeing one's reflected image on the mirror for what it is or observing a mountain by stepping away and keeping distance from it.

Some people use confession as a means to reduce suffering, just as clients with a fear of blushing confide their feelings to others. By sharing with and placing themselves in a third person's perspective, they reduce the weight of their mental burden and become more free from the suffering. Some people use poetry to describe their feelings and objectify themselves, thus lessening the pain and soothing their agony. However, these are specific means one can use to attain certain purposes. Be aware that means and purposes are not identical.

The reason that clients with *shinkeishitsu* constantly complain about their symptoms to family members is because they want others to acknowledge their suffering and give sympathy and special care to them. Paradoxically, this practice of complaining increases clients' suffering. The more they detail their complaints, the more they focus their attention upon the complaints. They become egocentric and conclude that they alone suffer while others are free from pain. Thus, they create a large gap between others and themselves, build a castle of egocentric emotions in which they confine themselves even more, and lose correct judgment regarding facts. This is a totally different psychological process than the act of confession and blatant self-disclosure.

Individuals with *shinkeishitsu* resent others who do not understand their condition. They talk about the positive feelings they hold toward others, but do not let others know their less desirable feelings because it might disadvantage their relationship. Those with *shinkeishitsu* do not normally face tribulation in a quiet and solitary manner. They do not expose themselves entirely and with objectivity; and they are unable to appraise themselves accurately from a third person's perspective. Rather, they use all their energy on futile attempts to avoid agony, multiply their suffering by envying others, and lament their adversity. I think they generate suffering and confusion because they fail to enter into either a totally subjective experience or take on a completely objective position. Instead, such individuals vacillate between the two perspectives in a middle stance and thus remain in suffering and confusion. I have discussed my observations from the perspective of contradiction by ideas.

Needless to say, the above points can also be discussed in terms of emotion and attention.

I would like to add a few explanations about contradiction by ideas. One becomes conflicted when s/he projects her or his experiences and subjective facts onto the external world as an objective model. It is similar to seeing one's face reflected on the surface of a mirror. Thoughts are reflected as surface images, and often show inaccurate, reversed images and contradictions. For this reason, when a person takes an idea for a fact, s/he becomes preoccupied with it. This is like a man who struggles to adjust the angle of a razor when he shaves his beard by using a mirror as his guide.

Clients with *shinkeishitsu* tend to get attached to a thought and force it into action as though it were reality. This produces idiosyncratic behaviors and contradiction by ideas. Herein, I advise my clients to use a thought as a guide while acknowledging its limited caliber for choosing action. This is comparable to using a mirror only to identify a certain spot on the face while relying on a natural hand movement to guide the razor. Similarly, clients who try many different ways to fall asleep only end up with insomnia; as they try to forget pain, they become even more attached to it. Also, as they forcefully attempt to suppress obsessive thoughts, they become more agonized by them. In essence, these experiences result from clients' preoccupation with the contradiction between ideas and reality.

People often deceive themselves by such contradiction by ideas. Clients with *shinkeishitsu* say, "I could cope with dying from another illness, but I don't want to die of this one (*shinkeishitsu*)," or "I would persevere with any other suffering, but can't stand this one." Also, those with mysophobia may find the agony that accompanies hand washing unbearable and say, "I'd rather cut off my hands." These remarks are the expressions of their contradiction by ideas by which they deceive their mind at the moment. They do not realize that they would reject most torment and would not want to die of any illness, regardless of its nature. In addition, these clients remain engaged in self-deception and self-defense due to the contradictions in their thinking. They use various excuses in order to seek comfort, maintain lazy behaviors, and avoid responsibilities.

Many people entertain beliefs similar to, "I would not mind dying after I reach seventy," or "I want to die quickly and in peace." They take these idealistic preferences for factual truth, and fail to notice that they are deceiving themselves. No one among such self-deceptive persons would be prepared to follow a self-instruction like, "Die suddenly, now." They prefer not to die now or ever.

A close relative of mine died at age one hundred and three. His children lamented his death while sitting beside his body. Some neighbors who witnessed this response laughed secretly at the family's emotional reactions because they believed the deceased person lived to such a rich old age. Yet, it is natural for humans to be saddened by death regardless of how long a deceased person had lived. Grieving is endless. Family members may wish for the dead person's presence during the next New Year's celebration, or during the great grandchildren's graduation ceremonies.

The prevalence of contradiction by ideas among people seems to be caused by the following processes: (1) a person forms an idea that is incongruent with reality; (2) s/he objectifies such ideas; (3) s/he projects these objectified ideas onto the external world; and (4) s/he expands the boundaries of her or his projected ideas. The perpetuation of these processes leads a person's mind astray and leads her or him farther away from reality. This sequence is known as *akuchi* (misplaced intellect) in Zen.

Obedience to Nature

It is essential that the therapist comprehend the importance of dismantling the clients' contradiction by ideas when treating those with *shinkeishitsu*. How can a client dismantle her or his methods of faulty thinking? In short, the solution lies in assisting a client to discard artificial tactics and manipulations and to observe and obey nature. Trying to control the self by manipulation and willpower is like trying to choose numbers willfully on a thrown dice or to push the water of the Kamo River in Kyōto upstream. As a result, the client aggravates the original agony and feels unbearable pain because s/he fails to get what was desired; hence, a sense of powerlessness increases.

What is nature? In Japan, it is natural that the summer is hot and the winter is cold. One is not in accordance with reality if one tries not to feel the summer's heat or the winter's cold. It is more natural to obey and persevere with the reality of the seasons. One day, a monk questioned Dōsan, a Zen master: "How can we avoid the arrival of heat and cold?" Dōsan answered: "Go to a place where hot and cold do not exist." The monk asked him to elaborate on this. He answered: "When it's cold, lose yourself in the cold. When it's hot, lose yourself in the hot." This means that one can immerse the self in a state of the hotness or coldness when it is hot or cold, respectively. One can, therefore, become oblivious to temperature, as in the saying, "Heat is also cool when one is in a mindless state." This is what I mean by "obedience to nature."

Fearing death, disliking discomfort, lamenting calamities, and complaining of that which one cannot control are all natural human responses and emotions. These are as natural as water flowing to a lower latitude. Also, one gets heaviness in the head after oversleeping, discomfort in the stomach after overeating, and heart palpitations when startled. These are also governed by nature's laws and cannot be exempted from the nature of causality. These phenomena cannot be manipulated to conveniently suit one's wishes. Therefore, one need only to obey nature.

The Opposing Function of Mind

Among humans' psychological activities, there is a phenomenon called the "opposing function," that is, the function of counterbalancing or self-harmonizing. The opposing function operates much like the movement of muscles. For example, the flexor muscle and the extensor muscle of the upper arm are called the opposing arm muscles. These arm muscles, when the arm is bent or stretched, work harmoniously and adjust their tension to create smooth movements.

Without this opposing muscle function, one's movements would be like that of a mechanical doll. When the muscles on both sides tense concurrently, the arm becomes tight and immobilized. When such muscles become over stimulated, they start shaking, develop spasms, and exhibit other reactions. When the muscles of one side become paralyzed or tightened, the arm will stiffen and remain in the same bent or stretched position. The mental function is understood in a similar manner.

Examples of the psychological opposing or balancing function are as follows: when one develops a fear, the opposing wish to not fear emerges; when one is showered with compliments, one surely thinks of things about her or himself that are undeserving of another's praise; when a person is rich, s/he worries about becoming poor; and when one desires to buy something, one also thinks of its wasteful nature. When a person goes out the front door, s/he looks at the door to see if it is closed. When someone hits a nail with a hammer, s/he uses both strong and weak muscle forces. These opposing and self-inhibitory processes are natural phenomena of human functioning. Neither the opposing function of the mind nor that of muscular movements is at the service of willful manipulation.

If a client's opposing function is deficient, then s/he develops uninhibited, impulsive behaviors as exhibited by infants and those with intellectual disabilities. When this function is paralyzed or slackened, a client may exhibit unmonitored and impudent statements and behaviors as shown by extreme drug or alcohol abuse, or certain types of psychotic disorders. However, when the self-inhibitory part of this function becomes too strong, one loses spontaneity in speech and action, as seen among depressed clients.

This also applies to people diagnosed with schizophrenia (catatonic type) when they develop mental agitation or delirium. Such phenomena are comparable to the alternate rigid cramping of muscles. The various sufferings and loss of spontaneity are due to an exaggerated tension between desires and inhibitions.

What Freud calls "repression" is also a phenomenon of the psychologically opposing function. For example, the opposing function is mobilized when sexual desire is accompanied by the thought that it is immoral and antisocial to have such a desire. Yet, it is normal that the sexual desire is different from other desires, such as the desire for food. Sexual desire is accompanied by a self-inhibiting response because of the socializing contexts in which people live, even though this is not necessarily the case with other animals. Therefore, we encounter various complex problems in living our lives as humans.

Freud (1896b) explains that hysteria and other neuroses are caused by the mechanism of repression of the sexual drive. Aside from a discussion of his strained interpretations, I believe that the cause of neurosis is not limited to the repression of the sexual drive. Rather, it is caused by the desire for life (*sei-no yokubō*) and the natural fear of death. The opposing function of sexual inhibition is a natural phenomenon that exists in all humans. Therefore, such a function of mental opposition can help therapists understand more clearly how, when, where, and in what kind of relationships inhibition operates in children, those with intellectual disabilities, and those with hysteria, *shinkeishitsu*, and other psychological disorders.

Some scholars explain the pathology of shoplifting by the term *split personality*. However, shoplifting can be explained by the mental opposition between the desire to obtain something and the awareness that stealing is an antisocial act. A person shoplifts for various reasons. For instance, one with hysteria behaves from the mental confusion that occurs during heightened emotion when one desires something; or one with an intellectual disability may act out of undeveloped inhibitions. Those with *shinkeishitsu* develop an obsessional fear of stealing due to an inner conflict arising from the psychological opposing function. If a therapist makes a diagnosis of split personality in a boy who exhibits antisocial behaviors, then s/he contends that the boy is acting by his first personality when he understands moral teachings and refrains from stealing. When the boy exhibits impulsive behaviors, he is acting by his alternate personality. And when he regrets his behavior, he is considered to have returned to his first personality. Such explanations, however, only becloud the actual psychological meaning of stimulus or drive.

When the first impact of a stimulus or impulse in the mind is strong, the self-inhibitory or fear-avoiding reaction is correspondingly very strong. Therefore, a person's torment can become increasingly stronger when the "contradiction by ideas" is operating, particularly in the presence of other complicated psychological conditions.

The opposing function is also manifested in a client's attempt to persevere when s/he wants something or feels scared; it may also occur in the various ways s/he denies desire. A person's denial of desire creates complicated inner conflicts regarding life problems. The degree to which the opposing function operates in a person is part of her or his natural human emotional process and reflects her or his level of psychological development.

Choice of Circumstance

The contradiction by ideas will diminish as one accepts the feelings of coldness, pain, fear, or agony as they are and does not use artificial and cumbersome tricks to eliminate these feelings. To accept one's feelings as they are implies obedience to nature, which is the absolute obedience to facts or truth.

Such an obedience to nature is the subjective attitude to be developed and fostered in clients through therapy. This attitude is necessary for therapists to adopt when applying my therapy, despite the fact that clients try to obtain an ideal state of mind. The methods and the conditions that assist clients to develop this attitude are quite a different matter. If clients contrive ways to obey nature or endeavor to achieve a "proper" attitude by themselves, then their activities are no longer natural. By contriving or endeavoring, one attempts to treat oneself objectively as a third person and subsequently ignores her or his real self. Therefore, what is required to achieve the natural psychological attitude is simply the choosing of external situations or circumstances. For example, one can make a firm resolution that surpasses life and death concerns only when one cuts off one's avenues of retreat. Similarly, it is not until a person experiences complete solitude that s/he realizes that others cannot be relied upon for sympathy or assistance. It is self-deceptive to imagine an extreme situation, or to speak about the importance of independence and self-reliance simply from one's intellect. One cannot obtain true courage or take determined actions only through imagination and discussion. This is more fully explained when I discuss my therapy for acute stress disorders.

Consider the following case that serves to represent this obedience to nature. A client complained of poor memory and comprehension. He stated that it was causing him great disappointment and pain and believed his symptoms were evidence of his declining brain function. When I asked him whether he had ever felt disappointment or pain with regard to his eyesight (nearsightedness), which is clearly a pathological abnormality, he replied that he had never felt this way. In replying so, he revealed his obedience to nature. He was ready to accept the inconvenience and annoyance of nearsightedness as integral to this condition. In contrast, he struggled to recover from a suspected decline of his brain function without seeking a medical evaluation to determine if it were an actual brain disease or definite abnormality. His agony and subsequent inner conflict arose from his anxious drive to fulfill his desire. However, theoretical persuasion is not always useful in treating clients.

Even the simplest theory will not necessarily be understood by the client, and even when the theory is understood, the pain may persist. In other words, since the client has an emotional preoccupation with her or his abnormal condition, any attempt to deny or remove this attachment contradicts the obedience to nature. It is only by means of providing the client with an appropriate ecological environment that destruction of her or his contradiction by ideas can be accomplished and the client can realize experientially the state of obedience to nature. It is not until clients master this state that they can be liberated from pain and agony. This is the foundation of my theory.

Emotion is subjective reality, while intellect leads one to assess objective reality. For instance, one's fear of death is an undeniable emotional fact, in the same way that one feels hot in summer and cold in winter. Similarly, abandoning an unfulfilled desire is no more possible than overcoming the fear of death. Only when one accepts this impossibility does one learn to obey absolutely these objective facts in external circumstances and become liberated from suffering.

Meaning of "Subjectivity"

Some explanation is necessary to define my meaning of the terms *subjectivity* and *experiential understanding*. The original meaning of these terms lies in the state itself, regardless of whether it is a sensation, mood, reaction, or behavior; understanding occurs in one's intuition or self-awareness itself, apart from objective appraisal. This idea is implied by the Zen term *shoichinen* (one's original intention) and by what CHIKASHIGE calls *ichidan ronpō* (one-step logic). Subjectivity is represented by a state in which one conducts business with nearsightedness, without observing or assessing it. Similarly, it is healthy, subjective behavior when a person eats according to her or his appetite without noticing where the stomach is located. It is abnormal to make a special assessment on one's state of discomfort or to express good feelings about the stomach. When a person observes "self" and comments on her or his health or abnormality, s/he is viewing the self objectively as a third person, and projecting the self onto the external environment for observation. From a subjective state, a person can confirm the presence of her or his head without physically observing the self or projecting an image of her or his self. It is only in this subjective state that one promptly avoids a stone thrown at her or his face. This ability comes from one's experiential embodied understanding (*taitoku*).

In contrast, objective observation occurs when one studies the shape of her or his face as shown in a mirror, or projects her or his self onto the external environment. When this occurs, a man cannot freely shave his face. We usually know that we are awake without the need for any "self" awareness; this is an example of the state of subjectivity. If we doubt whether we are awake or in a dream and try to prove it, then we become puzzled and confused. Even if we pinch ourselves and feel pain, we can never be convinced completely that we are not dreaming. Subjectivity and experiential understanding are free from doubt and confusion. Whereas objective observation is accompanied by doubt.

Lao-tzu stated that, "The principle of universal truth should be called 'nothingness' or 'namelessness.' However, once it is named 'nameless,' it loses its original identity." This passage represents the "subjectivity" to which I refer. When something is named, it becomes objective knowledge. This is quite difficult to explain. However, it can be understood only after experiencing my therapy for *shinkeishitsu*.

Attention

When a person performs instinctive or habitual acts for which s/he makes no intentional effort, s/he is not aware of where s/he places attention. In contrast, if an action is of critical value to a person's life, then s/he will remain aware and alert. One's daily activities proceed smoothly when stimulation, effort, and placement of one's attention are aligned. For example, a Japanese person picks up cooked beans with chopsticks easily and almost unaware, without paying any attention to the chopsticks or to making the effort. One does not think about how s/he manipulates the chopsticks. In contrast, when a Japanese person accepts a cup of sake from someone before whom s/he feels shy or humble, her or his fingers may tremble and s/he may drop the cup. This is because s/he does not place attention on the cup itself, but rather places attention on other things, such as the way s/he holds the cup, the way s/he poses the body, or the way s/he thinks. In other words, a person loses what I call the "peripheral feature of consciousness" when attention is not directed toward the objective. Instead, one pays unnatural and centripetal attention to her or his placement of the hands and feet or some other irrelevant feature. The harder one strives, the more difficult it becomes to control attention. Somehow, crossing a log bridge that is twenty feet high seems more difficult than crossing a bridge that is two feet high. When a bridge is only two feet high, we focus our eyes on a point we desire to reach; whereas, if a bridge is perceived as being too high, we focus our eyes between the direction we are going and the space under our feet. People who sleepwalk have been known to walk along the edge of a steep cliff because their attention is genuinely focused on the objective alone. They are in a state of self-oblivion and do not pay any attention to the placement of their feet.

Some clients with *shinkeishitsu* complain about feeling clumsy. For instance, a person may feel unsure about how to play the violin when s/he concentrates on finger placement. Similarly, a person may feel drawn toward a train when walking beside a railway track. Some complain that their finger movements are unnatural while writing, and may even experience spasms in extreme cases. All of these phenomena can be explained by the loss of the person's peripheral feature of consciousness. Moreover, when clients with mysophobia worry about their hands being dirty and pay excessive attention to their hands, their eyesight becomes blurred because of their intense scrutiny to discern cleanliness. This phenomenon is due to the extreme constriction of the muscles that regulate convergence of the eyes, loss of proper accommodation, and fatigue of the ocular muscles, which are somehow caused by the client's excessive attention and effort.

The peripheral feature of consciousness (*mushojū-shin*) is greatly exaggerated in states of extreme excitement, such as astonishment or anger. In such states, a client's unconscious attention is concentrated on the objective alone, and s/he totally forgets the self and the external environment. Thus, an excited state is accompanied often by the clouding of one's consciousness. In this condition, attention cannot be focused centrifugally, and miraculous feats may be achieved, as described by some clients with hysteria. This occurrence is totally opposite to the manifestation of *shinkeishitsu*.

Relationship between Attention and Consciousness

In explaining the relationship between attention and consciousness, I use an example of two clients (A and B) who experience fear of having seen a person with apoplexy (stroke). Suppose that in response to witnessing a stroke, client A experiences agoraphobia while client B experiences fixed partial paralysis. Client A exhibits a *shinkeishitsu* response when s/he fears going into crowded places like theaters or busy streets; the fear in this case is based on anticipation and is not accompanied by extreme excitement or clouding of consciousness. Consequently, when describing this phenomenon, I think it is more appropriate to use descriptive terms, such as "loss of consciousness phobia" or "heart-attack phobia," rather than general terms like agoraphobia. The partial paralysis of client B is symptomatic of hysteria. The witnessing of a stroke released the emotion of fear and induced clouding of consciousness which captured the client's attention; this led to fixed symptoms through a mechanism similar to hypnosis. In this way, *shinkeishitsu* is an intellectual and anticipatory fear while hysteria is a particular consciousness steeped in emotional activity. Given this view, I take contention with the theory of the sub-conscious. The present-day theories regard the subconscious as stationary states or consequences, whereas my theory aims at investigating the conditions or processes involved in the formation of symptoms. When I treat these abnormali-ties, I do not attach much importance to the notion of con-sciousness, but rather attempt to adjust the environmental conditions surrounding the onset of symptoms.

I have studied the symptoms of *shinkeishitsu* from the perspective of "disoriented attention." I believe that the therapy for these symptoms must include an attempt to re-cover the peripheral feature of consciousness through increas-ing a client's spontaneous mental activity. For example, the work stages of my therapy are designed to guide clients to spontaneous activity and to concentrate on the goals of the work so that they have no time to make self-observations.

It is important to note that once a symptom has been established in a client with *shinkeishitsu*, it becomes the fo-cus of her or his attention. Therefore, it is quite natural for the client to preoccupy her or himself with symptoms. This follows the logic of the peripheral feature of consciousness wherein the symptom is the natural circumstance to which the client adheres, suffers, and fears. It is unnatural for the client to attempt to deny or eliminate the symptom. In do-ing so, s/he would indulge in useless self-observation and be trapped in the contradiction by ideas. Thus, a psychologi-cal conflict between the target of attention and self-criticism would occur. It is, in this regard, better to have the client concentrate on the symptom and feel the pain. By doing so, s/he may gradually enter into the state of natural conscious-ness and stop experiencing pain.

For example, when I treat clients with the symptom of tinnitus that originates from *shinkeishitsu*, I advise them not to divert their attention from the tinnitus, regardless of what they are doing, such as reading, working, or engaging in con-versation. If they succeed in maintaining this constant atten-tion, they will learn to obey nature from experience and will become unaware of their attention. Thus, the persistent tinnitus is usually forgotten in a few weeks. However, clients often think that if they do what I have advised, the tinnitus will be aggravated and they will be unable to follow my advice. Consequently, it takes a long time for them to overcome the tinnitus because of these beliefs. The disappearance of tinnitus can be explained by the same phenomenon that occurs when people gradually cease to be aware of the ticking sound of a clock when in the presence of the sound.

Harmonizing Function of the Mind

The above-mentioned phenomenon can also be explained by the harmonizing function of the mind. We tend to be disturbed by external sounds (such as the sound of a carpenter hitting a tin plate), while we are not bothered by the same sound if we produce it ourselves (despite the fact that the self-imposed sound is closer to our ears). This contradiction occurs because we strain or relax our attention according to who hits the tin plate. Thus, the condition of our mind is in accord with the sound. If we voluntarily focus our attention on the noise from outdoors, our mind will soon be harmonized with the sound and we will soon be able to read or do calculations in the presence of the sound. Similarly, if we conform our body movements to the rolling of a ship, we will focus on our intentional attention at first, but will gradually lose awareness of the attention. When we are no longer aware of the rolling movement of the ship, we avoid seasickness. It is for this reason that we do not become seasick when we row a boat by ourselves. Similarly, we may feel as if we are drawn along a rapid stream while standing on a bridge over a stream because the movement of our eyes is not in harmony with the stream. However, we do not feel uncomfortable if we focus our attention and match the movement of our eyes with the speed of the water. When we travel by train, we are not aware that our body is moving because it moves at the same speed as the train. However, we experience a violent shock if the train stops suddenly. At that moment, the harmony of movement between the train and our body is broken. After our ears harmonize with the noise of the train going through the tunnel, we become intensely aware of the silence, as a soundless, negative sound when the train comes to a stop at a station. At this moment, the focus of attention to the sound is suddenly relaxed.

The relationships described above reflect the relativity of the association between the external environment and the self. The more harmonized the stimulus from the external environment and our attention becomes, the less aware we are of the stimulus. In contrast, the more we oppose the stimulus, the more intensely we feel it. Clients with *shinkei-shitsu* become oversensitive for the same reason without the operation of any organic mechanism. I have termed this occurrence "pseudo-hypersensitivity." Those with *shinkeishitsu* continuously resist external stimuli because of a morbid fear and their struggle to eliminate the stimulus. Since they dare not conform to the stimulus, they develop symptoms.

Mushojū-shin

The word *mushojū-shin* is used in Zen to describe healthy attention. It occurs when one does not limit her or his attention to a single focus and uses the mind fully. *Mushojū-shin* describes a state in which attention is not fixed on a particular point and the entire mind is alert and functioning; attention extends in all directions. While in this state, a person deals with a given situation immediately and appropriately. For instance, when standing in a moving train, we can sometimes read a book without holding a strap and without falling. We do not miss our transfer or have our pockets picked. The reason that we can respond appropriately to the changes in circumstances is that we are in the state of *mushojū-shin*. If we were to focus all our attention on any one of the above activities, we would surely experience some mishap. The condition of *mushojū-shin* can be achieved in a train by shifting one's weight onto one foot, keeping the other one in a rest position and calmly assuming a so-called *sutemi* (self-less) attitude, leaving ourselves open to anything. This body posture and mental attitude, though seemingly being in an unstable state, create an ideal state of mind=body. Therefore, the mind keeps itself in tension, responds to changes in external circumstances in a generally alert manner, and directs attention freely in such a state.

Symptoms of *shinkeishitsu* occur because the client's attention is fixed on her or his symptoms. My therapy for those with *shinkeishitsu* promotes spontaneous activity in the client's mind, directs her or his attention toward external circumstances, and removes narrowly focused attention. Hopefully, treatment will lead the client's state of mind to the state of *mushojū-shin*. This is the place from where my special therapy begins.

Guiding Principles of Emotions

An explanation of emotions may assist therapists in understanding my treatment. My therapy for clients with *shinkeishitsu* focuses on their emotions, rather than their system of logic or volition.

Principle One: When emotion is left to flow naturally, it assumes a parabolic course. It flares up, reaches a climax, then lessens and disappears.

For example, my experience with isolation-rest therapy demonstrates that pain and suffering gradually subside if one endures them and lets them follow a natural course. Ponder the old lesson from Tosa (the old name of Kochi Prefecture): "When one is angry and wishes to fight, think it over for three days before taking any action." This lesson supports the fact that an intense emotion will disappear naturally over the course of three days.

In addition, emotion subsides immediately when it is expressed. For example, sadness is alleviated by crying, and anger is reduced by shouting. Though this may be regarded as compensation, it can also be attributed to the natural course of emotion. William James (1922) regarded the emotion of sadness and its expression in an inverse way, saying that we do not cry because we are sad, but we are sad because we cry. However, I think that the emotion of sadness subsides with crying according to its natural course. I consider that the crying and the emotion of sadness are a single phenomenon. These different points of view arise from the interpretation one gives to emotion; emotion can be interpreted as either an objective or a subjective phenomenon.

The induction of catharsis for hysteria as discussed by Freud (1896b) is a method that assists clients to express their emotions and desires. According to Freud, fear is present during the accidental event that causes a condition. I regard Freud's method of analysis as a symptomatic therapy that uses my principles of emotion. Also, catharsis can be interpreted as an escape from the psychological burden of congested emotion. The process of catharsis is similar to the process of the confession method that Imamura proposed for psychological liberation.

Principle Two: Emotion rapidly decreases and disappears when impulses are satisfied.

This statement can be illustrated by the fact that hunger is eliminated by eating and passionate love is ended by marriage. When clients with *shinkeishitsu* experience feelings of pessimism or irritation, they often seek methods to escape the discomfort. In doing so, clients obtain temporary relief. Later, however, they suffer from rational self-reproach and experience incessant feelings of regret with increased sufferings. Under these circumstances, clients begin to realize that it is wiser to endure their emotions and restrain from expressing their impulses. In contrast, clients who are weak in volition also find relief by satisfying their impulses, but they lack the ability to regret their action or restrain their impulses through a sense of social sensitivity. The more they experience relief, the harder it is for them to control the expression of their impulses and emotions. In contrast, clients with *shinkeishitsu* are able to restrain their impulses.

Principle Three: Emotion becomes dulled and less worrisome when it is repeatedly stimulated by the same sensation.

As we get used to cold or heat, we become less sensitive to feeling these temperatures. If a child is scolded regularly, s/he will become completely accustomed to such reproaches and finally cease to pay attention to the scolding. The purpose of placing clients with *shinkeishitsu* in cold baths is to train them to endure the sensation of discomfort. If clients learn to endure discomfort, their exaggerated sense of pain will diminish. Certain methods of therapeutic treatment will either increase or decrease the experience of a client's emotions—depending on their understanding and application of these principles of emotion.

Principle Four: Emotion is intensified when the stimulus is incessantly given and when attention is focused on the emotion or stimulus.

Emotion becomes stronger when a person expresses it beyond its natural course. For example, quarrels between people become more intense when anger is continuously re-stimulated. Many quarrels can be prevented if one exercises caution to her or his first word of utterance at the beginning of conversation.

The more minutely clients with *shinkeishitsu* complain of their symptoms or pain to their family and friends, the more intensively they focus attention on their own symptoms. In addition, when they accuse others of lacking compassion, they aggravate their symptoms. For these reasons, from the beginning of my therapy, I prohibit clients from complaining about their symptoms to family members.

Principle Five: Emotions are learned through new experiences and cultivated by repetition.

We first learn the taste of something by eating or drinking it, and we become better at a hobby by practicing it. We can cultivate courage and self-confidence only through repeated experiences and successes. Through such processes, we become used to the pain that accompanies effort and we learn the pleasure of success. In contrast, we become more cowardly and self-debasing through repeated mistakes and failures when we focus on negative feelings associated with them.

(These emotional principles are carefully noted when I administer my experiential therapy for *shinkeishitsu*).

Considerations in the Treatment of Anxiety Disorders with a Hypochondriac Base (*Shinkeishitsu*)

My therapy for *shinkeishitsu* attempts to provide training and education for those who generate emotions from a hypochondriac base. Therapy is designed to assist clients to overcome the psychological processes that intensify their symptoms into a spiral-like motion. Treatment is designed to destroy clients' contradictions by ideas by pointing to the psychology of their attention and emotions. My therapy has a radical nature that constantly pushes clients to obey nature by means of actual proof and experiential understanding.

I do not emphasize suggestion therapy as does Charcot (1877), nor do I believe in miracles wrought by therapy. I no longer employ the mechanical life-control method of Binswanger (1911), and I do not treat my clients using persuasive arguments as does DuBois (1908). Moreover, I do not find it necessary to search in depth for circumstantial events that serve as causes to symptoms as does Freud (1916–1917). My therapy does nothing other than provide experiences that educate clients about nature and their lives, behaviors, emotions, and mental attitudes. Therapy uses methods that confront clients' pretherapy experiences; they learn how to evaluate and apply their experiences in daily living. Different methods are used for different symptoms of *shinkeishitsu*. I have designed the following special prescription for treatment to serve as a fundamental therapy for general *shinkeishitsu*, regardless of certain differences in the therapeutic intervention for the specific type of *shinkeishitsu*.

2 therapy for anxiety disorders with hypochondriasis (shinkeishitsu)

Origins of the Method of Treatment by Morita

Although I tried various therapies, including hypnosis for clients with anxiety disorders, I did not obtain results beyond the temporary relief of symptoms in clients. I also used the life-control method for many years and followed Binswanger's (1911) theory, only to find it manneristic, too theoretical, relatively impractical, and ineffective. Binswanger's methods deprived my clients of spontaneous activity. Initially, I tried to modify and extend these existing systems, but later designed my own method of treatment.

In principle, my method of therapy requires residential or hospital inpatient care for my clients. Treatment at a client's home is possible in very rare and select cases and requires daily diary writings upon which the therapist makes written comments. My treatment involves four stages: (1) isolation-rest therapy, (2) light occupational therapy, (3) heavy occupational therapy, and (4) complicated activity therapy in preparation for actual life. Treatment in the first and second stages is conducted with clients being placed in a completely isolated state; they are not allowed to have any social and family contact. Clients are permitted to go out of the hospital grounds for the first time in the fourth stage. The essential characteristics of my therapy are the natural treatment of the mind=body, and the experiential methods. USA Genyu from Kyōto once named my therapy as "self-awareness therapy."

The First Stage: Isolation and Rest

During this period, clients are placed in complete isolation and told to maintain a resting or prone state, except during use of the toilet and bath. Any activities that provide ways of distracting themselves (such as meeting with people, having conversations, reading, and smoking) are prohibited.

This method has several merits. First, therapists can observe the client's mental condition during rest and can use these observations for further diagnosis. Secondly, clients can recover from mental and physical fatigue through rest. The main purpose of this therapy is to radically dismantle the client's mental suffering and pain, and to let her or him experience the mental state that I call "immediate liberation through confrontation with one's suffering."

The inspiration for this stage comes from my clinical observations of how effective rest therapy is in treating my clients who manifest anxiety-based disorders. I have observed how pain and anxiety disappear through the natural course taken by an emotion when the client is left alone in a tranquil condition, without complicated external stimuli. I have read a collection of Buddhist sermons by the Zen priest, HAKUIN (1686–1769) about the method of introspection and the way to enlightenment and found that we hold similar ideas. However, the psychological explanations for my method are not related to religion.

Regarding diagnosis, clients with early-stage hebephrenia or mania are unable to observe the rules of rest therapy and may exhibit various symptoms of psychosis during the rest period. Only in rare cases do such clients remain in bed without any trouble. Clients with hysteria or a weak-willed disposition often fail to complete the rest therapy. Clients

Figure 3. Stage One of Morita Therapy: Isolation-Rest Room at Sansei Hospital, Kyoto, Japan (1992), (gratitude to Shin-ichi Usa, MD). Photo by John Maggiora.

with genuine *shinkeishitsu* follow the rules precisely and are always able to complete therapy.

Sudden Liberation without Tampering

It goes without saying that the course of rest therapy varies from person to person. In typical cases on the first day of treatment, clients are removed from external stimuli and lie down comfortably in a mentally and physically quiet state. Initially their appetite for food increases.

On the second day of rest, clients begin to wander in their thoughts because they do not suffer objective physical pain that accompanies physical diseases. They think about their personal affairs, discomforts, their past or future, and frequently experience doubts about their lives or have pessimistic thoughts about their future. Thus, they experience mental pain, anguish, and anxiety. Initially I tell my clients that "Although you suffer from unpleasant illusions or anxieties, do not attempt to divert your mind or try to escape the pain." I tell them to let their illusions or suffering run a natural course and to dare themselves to experience the pain. Even when the pain seems unbearable, I tell them to endure it, much like enduring a toothache or stomachache. In order to be relieved from suffering, it is better to endure discomfort rather than suppress it with the power of reason or thought.

Anxiety and suffering originate primarily from a person's mental denial or suppression of desire for the fulfillment of what s/he wants to attain or perform, specifically when the desire is inimical to the self or goes against conventional social values. In other words, anxiety is caused by a conflict between the opposing forces of desire and fear. The person experiences suffering from the pain associated with this conflict and becomes further entangled in various complicated ideas.

If clients with *shinkeishitsu* and obsessive or compulsive disorders experience pain and fear just as they exist (just as children and those with intellectual disabilities tend to do), these experiences will not change into anxiety. Clients double their pain when they focus on their constant anticipation of fear. Moreover, their suffering is tripled because they struggle anxiously not to experience the fear or pain. For example, if an infant of less than six months old undergoes surgery without anesthesia, s/he cries when the body is cut with the scalpel but ceases crying when surgery is over. The situation is not so simple for intellectually developed adults because of their anticipatory fear.

As a saying in Zen teaches: "If one tries to eliminate a wave with another wave, one will invite numerous waves." Similarly, when people strive to remove their pain and agony, they try to eliminate a wave in their minds with yet another wave; their minds inevitably become more confused and disturbed. Any attempt to control the mind can be likened to a person trying to lift her or his body alone by will power without the use of support.

During the period of isolated rest, clients frequently toss about on futon (bed) because of their anguish. Nevertheless, the more intensely the client suffers, the more s/he achieves the aims of treatment. When a client's agony reaches a climax, it naturally and completely disappears within a short time, just like victory can be achieved during the last five minutes of a dashing attack. A client's mind is suddenly refreshed as intense pain suddenly vanishes. I term this "immediate liberation through experiencing untampered suffering." This situation is not achieved intellectually but is caused by the sudden disappearance of "pathological emotion" through the process of one's natural emotional functioning. Clients usually experience this sudden change within only a few hours. In some cases, however, the agony does not appear in a definite form but occurs irregularly; it sometimes persists until the fourth or fifth day of treatment. If a client distracts or comforts her or his self by smoking or going out on the verandah, paradoxically, s/he postpones the moment of liberation. I call this stage "the agony period."

By the third day, the agony suffered by the client on the previous day disappears and will not reoccur, even if s/he tries to experience it again. The client will recollect with interest what happened to her or him the previous day and feel better about her or himself. People often enjoy the memory of hardship, such as that of mountain climbing or a forced march; they become encouraged and more confident by their own past feats. In the same manner, clients recollect their experiences of overcoming suffering and feel invigorated.

Through such experiences, I let my clients know that it is impossible to voluntarily develop the past emotion of fear or anxiety unless proper conditions are provided. Nor can such emotions be denied or removed by an ideology. For instance, we cannot be genuinely surprised by design or intention, and we cannot avoid being afraid of something that we fear.

The Stage of Boredom

On the fourth day, clients are liberated from their previous passive pain. The pain changes into another state and clients suffer from boredom and want to become active. I term this "the stage of boredom."

Healthy minds do not tolerate boredom; thinking and acting simply occur. Children show incessant movement and young people crave mental and physical activities. They cannot help being active. In contrast, as people advance into old age, they often desire less constant physical activity.

If a young client does not show any desire for action and is not bored at all, there are three possible explanations: (1) that the client is accustomed to confinement or lying down for long periods of time, (2) that s/he may be in an early stage of schizophrenia, or (3) that s/he has a weak-willed disposition. I refine my treatment by assessing the client during this stage of boredom. After facilitating methods that push my clients to fully experience the pain caused by their lack of activity, I move them out of the isolation bedrest on the following day and begin their second stage of therapy. The first stage usually lasts four to seven days.

Insomnia

Isolation-rest therapy is notably effective for *shinkeishitsu* symptoms that are accompanied by insomnia and anxiety. Insomnia in clients with *shinkeishitsu* originates from their fear of insomnia and is different from actual insomnia. Clients insist that they have not slept at all, even after they have slept quietly for some time. Some of them complain of insomnia for several months' duration.

I treated a man who worked as a barber; he claimed that he had not slept at all for three years because he had been working incessantly to earn his living. His insomnia, however, could be explained from a psychological perspective and I interpreted it as a subjective phenomenon. This client thought that his "unconscious" period of profound sleep occurred for only a brief moment; also, he experienced the period of marginal sleep (described as being half asleep and half awake) to be much longer than it actually was. Generally, sleep occurs in people when mental activities cease and they are free from all ideas and thoughts; this state renders them totally oblivious. Consequently, clients cannot fall asleep when they try hard to sleep because their minds are alert to their goal. In addition, such clients often try various tricks to induce sleep, only to find that their minds become more active. Sleeping becomes increasingly more difficult when anticipatory anxiety is aroused. Those who are indifferent to insomnia may sometimes become totally free from all thoughts and ideas as if they are asleep, although they may not actually be sleeping. We can observe children who wake up and go to the toilet at night; they often forget this activity and think they have slept through the night.

For these reasons, in treating the insomnia in clients with *shinkeishitsu*, I do not use Ziehen's (1908) method of instructing them to calm the mind gradually by alternately doing exercises and resting before going to bed. And though I have tried various methods of concentration, I no longer apply them to my therapy. These methods are not useful as a fundamental treatment for eradicating client's fears of insomnia.

I advise my clients to sleep whenever they want during the isolation-rest period, regardless of the time of day. I tell them that they do not have to worry even if they do not sleep for a week, and I prevent them from making any effort to sleep. In response, their fear of insomnia is broken and the pain associated with insomnia usually disappears within three to seven days. Also, clients become free from encumbered situations, like sleeping during the daytime and staying awake at night.

In addition to insomnia, those with *shinkeishitsu* often worry about their frequency of dreams. I have already stated that clients think they have an abnormal number of dreams when they fixate attention on their dreams and their fears. Self-observation shows that people remember dreams that occur in a shallow dream state. The only difference between those who claim they do not dream and those who complain to have too many dreams is that the former are indifferent to their dreams, while the latter place attention on their dreams.

The Second Stage: Light Occupational Work

The therapy in this stage is also conducted with the client in an isolated state. Conversation and amusements are prohibited. Sleeping is limited to seven or eight hours a night, and the client is instructed to go outdoors into the fresh air and sunlight during the daytime; s/he is not allowed to stay in the room to rest. The client is instructed to write in a diary after evening meals so that the therapist can better understand the client's physical and mental conditions. Moreover, twice a day, after washing her or his face in the

Figure 4. Stage Two of Morita Therapy: Wood Carving, Takehisa Kōra's private hospital, Tokyo (1992), (gratitude to the late Dr. Kōra, MD). Photo by John Maggiora.

morning and before going to bed at night, clients are told to read aloud a certain number of pages from the beginning of books such as the *Kojiki* (Records of Ancient Matters). The client need not understand the author's meaning; the process is more like reciting Buddhist scriptures. Through such readings, clients gradually resume mental activity, enliven themselves in the morning, and gradually dismiss disturbing thoughts and mental ruminations at night.

During the first and second days in stage two of treatment, any actions that use extensive muscles, including looking up at the sky, climbing stairs, or sweeping with a broom are prohibited. In addition, clients are not allowed to do anything to divert their minds or amuse themselves. For instance, going for a walk, exercising, whistling, singing, and playing with children or dogs are not allowed. Clients are to maintain a serious mental attitude and ride their physical discomfort and any obsessive ideas calmly and with patience—just as they are. They are encouraged to tidy the yard and perform small tasks such as picking up fallen leaves in the woods, weeding the garden, or removing withered leaves from the ground bamboo. They may make observations on ants or plants if they wish.

Prompting Spontaneous Activity

The purpose of the activity stage is to let the client calmly endure her or his distressful symptoms and to stimulate spontaneous activities and desires for action by driving the client to experience mental and physical boredom. Therapists are not to impose particular tasks on the client. In contrast, conventional occupational therapy assigns tasks and work periods to clients in a mechanical way and thus ignores clients' natural tendencies toward spontaneous activity.

Just as Montessori (1909) believes that spontaneous activity is highly effective in fostering education in children, so my therapy is designed to promote the desire for spontaneous activity in my clients. For example, therapy can be designed to stimulate the appetite in clients who suffer from malnutrition. I allow my clients to skip either breakfast or lunch if they claim they do not have an appetite, and I prohibit them from taking snacks. In this way, clients gradually desire three meals a day and appreciate food when they are hungry. People with extravagant eating habits do not realize the pleasure of a simple meal; a single bowl of rice with a slice of radish is very tasty.

The boredom induced by my second stage of therapy prompts clients to readily carry out activity that may have seemed useless to them in the past. As a client cleans part of a ground bamboo, s/he may find the other part is dirty and continue further to find new things to do, such as clearing away cobwebs or removing harmful insects from flower beds. Upon finding a nest of ants, the client may be driven by curiosity to examine it thoroughly. Thus, the client begins to show signs of perfectionism when engaging in activity, even though initially s/he thought the task was trivial. The desire to attain perfection is stimulated easily in clients with *shinkeishitsu*. In fact, it is from this desire for perfection that obsessive disorders often develop.

One does not become interested in a task unless one actually begins the task. Interest occurs for the first time when one acts. It is like hating a particular food without ever tasting it. One comes to love a certain food only when one actually eats it.

If a large task is imposed on the client (such as cleaning the entire yard), s/he will think about completing the task because of her or his perfectionist tendencies. The client will become overwhelmed by the anticipatory desire for success, begin to think about the difficulty of the task, and focus on the fear of failure. In response to this process, the client becomes incapable of starting the task. Those with *shinkeishitsu* tend to spend considerable effort allotting time for a task and estimating the amount of work involved. They exaggerate the difficulty of carrying out the work, feel burdened and troubled, and become irritated. Consequently, it is crucial when treating those with *shinkeishitsu* that the therapist break down clients' anticipatory fears by pointing to their respective experiences.

If clients ponder over the type of work that will be effective for their condition, or search around for activities to distract themselves from their suffering, they will suffer even more when they are unable to find suitable work. Moreover, if clients intentionally try to arouse their own interest and concentrate on becoming more attentive, their work activity will become impractical and they will be less able to apply themselves to it. Therapists are advised to keep this process in mind and to guide clients to begin their work immediately without allowing time for contemplation.

Breaking Down the Feeling-Centered "Attitude"

My therapy is designed to assist clients to stop evaluating their symptoms, methods of therapy, and the therapist's remarks so that their condition can run its natural course. During treatment, my clients often feel as if they are being deceived and wonder how their severe distress can be treated by such trivial methods. Usually these thoughts occur during the first isolation-rest period and the early period of light work therapy. During these initial periods, clients can be as doubtful as they like. They need not believe in the therapeutic process. Therapists are misguided when they think that effective results cannot be obtained unless their clients believe in the treatment. One's most profound understanding occurs through personal experience. Once clients experience the treatment, they trust it.

From the second day of stage two, clients are instructed to find work activity at night, such as sharpening toothpicks, sewing dust cloths, or making envelopes. They are not allowed to rest after meals, eat snacks, or lie down, except for seven or eight hours for sleep. They are forced into constant activity for sixteen or seventeen hours a day. Although this may sound like severe penance to some people, clients have scarcely complained about the intensity of this therapy, particularly because the environment provides natural stimulation. Only rarely do clients complain of lumbago (backache) that results from their squatting posture during the first and second days of this stage of treatment.

Following the third or fourth day in stage two, clients are allowed to do light manual labor, such as using a broom or a dust cloth. Restrictions on work are gradually relaxed, and work that uses more muscles is encouraged. Over time, clients become more active. In the same way as children feel joy in expressing their impulses, clients are liberated from their anticipatory fear and begin to enjoy the work itself. The work also becomes more diversified; clients begin to boil rice, cook food, heat the bath, clean the toilet, clear a ditch, or wash clothes, depending on the situation. In the evening, they may learn how to sew a simple kimono. Clients are encouraged to try work they have never done or learned, regardless of their social status, gender, or lifestyle. When clients seek more difficult work, which is naturally driven by the impact of their improving health, treatment moves on to the third stage. The second stage can last for one or two weeks, but there are no clear borders between stages.

Therapists deal with clients' complaints of pain by generally ignoring them; clients are left to deal with their complaints alone. At the end of the second stage, clients stop reporting their symptoms such as heaviness in the head, poor concentration, lethargy, stomach atony, and constipation. In order to dismantle the client's inclination toward self-examination, the therapist discourages the client from reporting on her or his condition. However, if clients report that their headache has disappeared and they feel refreshed, the therapist explains that such a feeling is nothing but an expression of self-awareness. Regarding the conditions for treating this disorder, these reports are not different from the reported feelings of pain. Comfortable feelings are always accompanied by an opposite uncomfortable feeling. Health in the true sense can be achieved only when one is free from the sensations of comfort and discomfort. The stomach is healthy only when one has no feeling in the stomach. Methods that promote spontaneous activity in a client's mind and body are generated in the second stage. My therapy transcends symptom-based therapies that concentrate on clients' subjective symptoms. My therapy aims at radical treatment and breaks down clients' self-evaluating attitudes by de-emphasizing a focus on feelings of comfort and discomfort.

The Third Stage: Intensive Occupational Work

During the third stage, therapists assign the client more labor-intensive work according to the client's physical condition, such as sawing and chopping wood, or working in the fields and digging holes. This stage of treatment assists clients (1) to acquire patience and to endure work, (2) to cultivate confidence in one's self and to empower subjective experiences, and (3) to provide encouragement through repeated experiences of success.

During the third stage, the therapist's attention is given to the dissolution of clients' anticipatory fears and their values about work. Clients are encouraged to do anything that they think normal people do. Since clients with *shinkeishitsu* are likely to have a strong desire to attain exceedingly high evaluation for their work, they harbor intense anticipatory feelings about their activities. The high sense of dignity and concern for vain appearance in these clients can be broken down by having them do work they think is below them, such as changing *geta* (Japanese clog) straps or cleaning excrement from toilets. In the same way that children express their impulses through lively activity, clients will find ways to exercise their mental functions and invent ways to work with their own efforts. In so doing, clients acquire the self-confidence that they can do anything others can do; they become gratified with their results and maintain an interest in their own work. Thus,

Figure 5. Stage Three of Morita Therapy: Chopping Wood, Takehisa Kōra's private hospital, Tokyo (1992), (gratitude to the late Dr. Kōra, MD). Photo by John Maggiora.

through their own direct experiences, clients learn to appreciate the value of labor.

There is an account of an officer of high public status whose wife was distraught because she heard that her husband was cleaning the floor and boiling rice. After he was restored to health and discharged from the clinic, I heard that he assisted his wife in realizing the value of labored work.

A client showed great ingenuity and made a violin with candy boxes and other pieces of wood considered useless. He succeeded in producing a beautiful sound from this crafted instrument. The joy of this client, felt at the moment he heard the instrument's sound, can be compared with the experience of Thomas Edison the moment he found a dim light emanating from his electric lamp. It is said that Edison was filled with ecstasy and just stared at the light for a long time and forgot about himself. This particular client told me that many people praised his violin, but no one understood his joy the way I did (as his therapist).

Such joy does not depend on the practical value of the product; the joy is in the subjective experience brought about because something has been achieved beyond expectation through one's own great effort. And the less one expects initially, the greater one's joy. Such experiences foster a subjective attitude in the client that invigorates her or his self to endure pain, overcome difficulty, and engage in lively and spontaneous mental and physical activities. The experiential understanding of confidence and courage, represented by the idea that much is possible in life, can be regarded as a kind of spiritual enlightenment. This experience cannot be attained by theory or thought. It is because of this attitude that a servant can become a spiritual leader or, like Mendel, a priest can find the science of heredity.

During the third period of treatment when clients are engaged in labor-intensive work, they experience the feeling of being incessantly busy. Therapists take these clients' feelings as a criterion from which to initiate the fourth stage of treatment. The goals of the third stage of treatment can usually be achieved in one or two weeks, although the duration differs according to each client. When I was developing my treatment, I assigned readings to clients at the beginning of the third stage of therapy; however, I have recently started to assign readings at the beginning of the fourth stage.

The Fourth Stage: Preparation for Daily Living

In the third stage, therapy concentrates on fostering the natural interests of the client. Clients act on the basis of their personal interests and are trained to achieve the power of endurance through activity. In contrast, training in the fourth stage aims to break all attachments, including fixation on one's own interests. Clients are trained to adjust to changes in external circumstances. This stage prepares clients to return to a rhythm of natural activity. During this period, the therapist encourages the client to read books and go outdoors solely for the purpose of doing errands.

Books for entertainment and those associated with ideological matters, such as philosophy and literature, are not included in this stage. Simple, realistic, descriptive, scientific materials about subjects in the areas of zoology, astronomy, history, and biography are given. Clients are not allowed to read alone in their rooms. They are told to read when they are tired of work, after meals, or simply when they feel like reading. Like Ninomiya Sontoku, they are encouraged to read at any time and many times a day repeatedly, as if they do not want to waste even a minute of their lifetime without reading. The prescribed way of reading is to open the book to any page at random and read silently without making any special effort to understand or remember the content. The amount of reading can be a mere few lines. They can stop at any time. If they want to read more, they will not be interrupted.

Generally speaking, clients with *shinkeishitsu* tend to complain constantly about their reading ability; they believe that their comprehension and memory have declined, or that they are distracted and unable to concentrate. However, this condition is not based on neurasthenia; it is self-induced by their anticipatory desire to read more effectively and their desire for perfection. Clients do not concentrate on the reading activity; rather, they examine their own feelings or speculate about things in the future (which only serves to increase their frustration).

As used in my therapy, reading trains clients to decrease anticipatory emotions that arise from their values and perfectionist character. Through therapy, clients begin to read calmly in just a few days, despite noisy places similar to those found in trains. They can read at any time—during spare time, at work, or even when they do not feel well—regardless of the difficulty of the book. Surprisingly, they sometimes enjoy themselves when they become absorbed in reading. Obsessive thoughts that surround the fear of reading can be cured easily, beyond all expectation, by simply reading in this way.

Clients are permitted to go out of the hospital for practical purposes, such as shopping for food. Going for a rambling walk or going outside just to see how they feel is not allowed. During purposeful outings, clients experience various mental states because they are exposed to the general world after a long period of isolation. One client with erythrophobia went to a grocery store in work clothes and realized that he had accomplished his errand smoothly, without any anticipatory fear. Similarly, clients who have been afraid to go outdoors because they fear a heart attack, often forget their fears naturally in this stage.

Pure Mind

During therapy, I take careful attention to foster clients' understanding of the "pure mind." Pure mind is their original and natural intrinsic disposition; it requires a mental attitude that does not deceive the self. Pure mind refers to "natural emotion" and an attitude that does not deny or cover up the reality of emotions. As one acts on the basis of this reality, one can develop her or his real self. A person does not need idealistic standards of right and wrong as a means to adjust actions to these standards. Also, one need not take a feeling-centered approach to please or satisfy her or his mood. When a person regards a task with reluctance and considers work as troublesome, quite voluntarily s/he makes an attempt to do the work more easily, quickly, and effectively. When Thomas Edison was working as a postal clerk, he invented a simple cart because he did not want to carry heavy packages. When he was a conductor on a train, he invented an alarm clock because he did not want to waste time waiting for his shift. These are the kinds of things that can be accomplished by a pure mind. In contrast, people who are idealistic think that they should try hard and persevere, that they should always like what they do, and that their lives should be trouble free. Consequently, their mental energy is wasted by their impossible attempts to avoid feelings of displeasure or boredom, and they fail to advance their self-development.

For example, a person sometimes hates someone else because of a bias or prejudice s/he holds; whereas, when the mind is pure, one is conscious of her or his prejudice and irrationality, develops compassion toward the other person, and gradually finds some virtues in him or her. In contrast, if a person tries to mold the self to the ideal that one should love everybody and hate no one, conflict between one's natural feelings and one's ideal images occurs and s/he tries to achieve the ideal; this process increases the person's anguish and eventually makes her or him even more sensitive to defects in other people.

Moreover, if a person breaks a plate by mistake, s/he may try to join the pieces of the plate together. This is a natural response to the accident and indicates one's regret. If one is in a state of pure mind, one is not trapped by her or his feelings of regret, and the next time s/he handles dishes s/he recollects suddenly the experience of breaking the plate and becomes more aware of safe handling. In contrast, after breaking the plate, if one worries about whether s/he will be scolded or ridiculed by others, apprehension will persist. In this agitated mental state of tension, one will try to be careful and sure-minded when handling the dishes. The persisting nervous and restless condition leads the mind to think, "I should be careful and stable." In this case, the person is more likely to repeat the same mistake. It is this kind of mental condition that leads a person with a swollen finger to hit the injured finger with a hammer despite efforts to protect it from pain.

Imagine, for instance, that a rabbit entrusted to your care is accidentally killed by a dog. If you have a pure mind, you will feel remorse for the rabbit, regret its death, and dislike the dog. If you think that you did not fulfill your care-giving responsibility and worry about whether another person will judge you as being careless, irresponsible, or indolent, then you will become a victim of your own misdirected thinking. If you think in this way, you may hate the whole experience and decide never again to take care of rabbits. In contrast, a pure mind realizes that accidents happen in spite of one's carefulness. In this way, a person becomes less anxious, is more inclined to care for rabbits, and becomes more creative in finding ways to keep animals safe.

It is difficult to explain the difference between the pure mind and the misdirected intellect simply through words because actual experience is required. The pure mind can be experienced only when clients are liberated from troublesome and uneasy relationships with others, ideals of right and wrong, and fixed prejudices—and when they are genuinely themselves. This state of mind is often experienced during one's secluded stage of treatment and is further developed in a gradual way during the four stages of this therapy.

3 the effectiveness of morita therapy

The Effectiveness of Morita Therapy

I have treated more than 260 clients by my hospitalization therapy from 1919 to 1928. The effects of this therapy are outlined in my work *Shinkeisuijaku-shō oyobi Kyohakukannen no Konjihō* (*Radical Treatment of Neurasthenia and Obsessive Ideas*); this includes results of treatment by USA Genya, MD. of Sansei Hospital in Kyoto. This volume also describes the treatment of clients who have a fear of blushing, and a case of complete recovery in a twenty-eight-year-old man. Though he had received other therapeutic treatments, he had been unable to study for nine years because of *shinkeishitsu* symptoms. Prior to my therapy, he had lost all hope of cure.

Process of Recovery

When *shinkeishitsu* symptoms are healed by my four-stage therapy, the client rarely recognizes when improvement began. This is like being unaware of the moment we fall asleep or being unable to remember when we forgot something.

Consider the case of a twenty-four-year-old farmer who had scarcely been able to eliminate without the use of laxatives for ten years. Recent treatment of more than five months in the department of gastroenterology failed to produce any positive effects. During the first ten days of my therapy, he had no bowel movements; I left this untreated. Thereafter, the client began to eliminate gradually. Forty days after hospitalization he showed spontaneous elimination in most three-day intervals. He was discharged from the hospital with other *shinkeishitsu* symptoms also healed. During the course of my treatment, it is common for symptoms of gastric atony to disappear from the client's preoccupation by the end of the second stage. However, constipation often needs a longer recovery period than gastric atony.

Shinkeishitsu symptoms often become very severe. Consider a fifty-one-year-old transportation business agent who had undergone long-term administration of Salvarsan injections following a misdiagnosis of syphilitic neurasthenia. The client consulted fifty-two physicians within five years after the onset of his symptoms; he solicited every conceivable kind of treatment by nonphysicians.

His major symptoms included vertigo and paroxysmal palpitation. When I visited this client, he had been confined on his futon (bed) to rest for a long time and he had many ups and downs in his condition. The client could not lift his head to eat, and he was constantly attended by one of four nurses who worked in shifts. After two and one-half months of hospitalization under my therapeutic treatment, he was able to work a full day. For more than seven years since my treatment, he has been actively working with no relapse. In this particular case, there was no relationship between the neurological symptoms and the positive Wassermann reaction on the client's blood test.

There have been numerous clients who have endured extended passive treatments after being diagnosed with dementia with no prospect of recovery; however, they achieved complete health as a result of my four-stage therapy and were able to lead active lives.

A sixty-eight-year-old woman had symptoms that consisted of vertigo, palpitation, insomnia, headache, and tinnitus; she was given the diagnosis of arteriosclerosis by another physician. Prior to my treatment, she was confined on her futon and received constant care, day and night, from two or three nurses for over four years. It may appear cruel to perform my isolation-rest therapy without any nursing care on such a client, but an accurate re-diagnosis justified applying my radical treatment. Also, this client voluntarily agreed to my treatment (though many female clients cry for the first several days of therapy because of their separation from their family). This client was hospitalized in January. And in spite of the fact that chilly winter weather limited her activity and she caught a cold virus, she was discharged about four months after admission. She returned to her normal activities.

Healing in Clients with Chronic Organic Dysfunction

During the course of my four-stage therapy, I have restored clients to a normal body temperature from low-grade fevers of 37.3C (99.14F) to 37.2C (98.96F) that were associated with infiltration in the pulmonary apex; also, I have cured proteinuria due to chronic nephritis. For clients with suspected physiological disorders, I usually ask Dr. HIROSE (whose opinion I trust) to perform a medical examination; we discuss the proper amount of exercise to be allowed for each client.

Consider a fifty-four-year-old woman who had continuously taken drugs for chronic nephritis (inflammation of the kidneys) for over nine years. One year previously, she developed secondary symptoms following the flu (palpitation, vertigo, insomnia, headache, constipation, and hypersensitivity of the foot, secondary to flu) and she was unable to leave her futon. She underwent hospitalization on a couple of occasions. This client cried for the first few days after being admitted to the hospital for my therapy. For the first week, she had constipation but was not given laxatives. The results of four urinalyses failed to reveal proteinuria. It is regrettable that I did not record the on-going healing process of her nephritis; her urine was not closely monitored for the first several weeks. However, following two months of therapy, all the symptoms disappeared and she was discharged.

A twenty-two-year-old male student with a fear of blushing developed nephritis following pleurisy and pulmonary infiltration at the age of nineteen years. On admission to our hospital, he showed obsessional thinking, and chronic nephritis with high levels of urinary protein. Following his medical examination, Dr. Hirose instructed him to perform only mild exercise and not to bathe. During his stay in the hospital, he became increasingly active and did hard work, such as chopping wood and heating water for bathing. About one month later, his urinary protein level was lower and two months after admission only traces of proteinuria were found by tests with sulfosalicylic acid; he was discharged with a complete recovery. More than one year has passed since this client's discharge; he is healthy and doing satisfactorily in his studies.

The cases described above are naturally of benign nephritis. Although I am not a specialist in this field, I invite scholars to study thoroughly the effects of treatment with isolation-rest therapy followed by gradual physical exertion for these chronic diseases.

In addition, I have experienced gradual healing in clients with empyema (inflammation of the nasal passages), hypertrophic rhinitis and the like, who were admitted to our hospital despite a specialist's recommendation for surgery.

Course of Treatment

Whether clients have ordinary *shinkeishitsu* or an obsessional disorder, they are restored to health by my therapy in the same time frame, regardless of the duration of the course of illness. One of my recovered clients claimed that he had been sick for twenty-five years, and two clients claimed they were sick for twenty-two years. Clients with *shinkeishitsu* who have personality disorders are difficult to treat regardless of the length of their illness. Recovery is also difficult in elderly people who live an inactive life and have little desire to sustain treatment. In contrast, those who have been inappropriately treated by other therapeutic methods have been readily cured by my method, even if they have had a long history of disorder. This may be comparable to an old saying, "Where there is great doubt, there is great enlightenment."

Clients with *shinkeishitsu* recover by eliminating their fixated attention on their subjective symptoms (which is a basic feature of their condition). Therefore, if clients try to cure themselves, their symptoms become aggravated because they are the focus of their own attention. This is similar to the outcome that occurs when a person directs her or his attention ever more intensely on something because s/he wants to forget it.

Adverse Effects of Conventional Methods of Treatment

The apparent effects of methods of treatment that use injections or electrical therapy* result largely from masked suggestion. These therapies are aimed at symptoms and only provide temporary management.

In clients subjected to symptom-based therapeutic procedures, a temporary positive effect is observed after the third to fifth administration of treatment. However, as the treatment is successively repeated, it becomes less effective and

---

*The electrical therapy used in Japan in the 1920s was not the same as electroconvulsive therapy (ECT), and there were no side effects such as memory impairment or neurological damage. As an historical note, Corletti and Bino invented ECT in Italy in 1938; independently, YASUKŌCHI and MUGASA developed ECT in Japan in 1939. Since MORITA died in 1938, he had no knowledge of ECT in his life time.

produces no cure. The negative effects of these therapeutic methods lie in the fact that clients become disappointed and attempt various other types of treatment when initial ones are ineffectual; this intensifies their morbid thinking. I have recognized ocular neurasthenia (as described to me by Dr. MAEDA) in only a few clients. I think his method of treatment concentrates solely on symptoms and does not provide a complete recovery for those with *shinkeishitsu*. In fact, he presented some clients in his book as having achieved a complete cure by his method; however, these same clients came to me for further care.

Other therapeutic methods, including popular psychotherapy, abdominal breathing, and psychic concentration on health (a form of auto suggestion in which the client concentrates on being healthy), cause contradiction by ideas in clients when they try to cure themselves or rid themselves of obsessional thinking. When the client is overly concerned with various treatments, preoccupation will merely cause the client to be further engaged in her or his disorder.

In treating *shinkeishitsu*, even if a client has a physically hypersensitive condition, therapists need to be cautious not to misdiagnose a client with a physically weak constitution as having neurasthenia. Indiscriminate application and continuous administration of sedatives, confined rest, or inactive or indulgent schedules is contraindicated in treatment.

A twenty-year-old student complained of intractable insomnia for one year. A physician advised him to withdraw from school temporarily and to rest; the physician believed the student would become physically weak as a result of continued study. In contrast, I told the client that a year of absence from school would reinforce the disorder rather than heal it; also, he might regret such a choice later. After eleven days of hospitalization with my therapy, the client was told to continue his study. As a result, he achieved an excellent academic record, was cured of his disease, and developed greater self-confidence and courage. Such a radical difference in therapeutic outcome occurred because the previous prescribed treatment was concerned only with the client's symptoms; physicians failed to comprehend the true essence of the man's illness.

Once the true nature of the symptoms in *shinkeishitsu* is understood, it is obvious that there is no benefit from the various types of injection therapy in current use. Even if calcium therapy has positive effects on the sympathetic nerves, exogenous substances injected into the body briefly circulate in the blood and are soon excreted. If such a treatment is made for the purpose of improving the physical constitution, it requires long-term injections of calcium. Calcium, however, can be ingested through ordinary foods. In addition, opium therapy, which has been used in treating obsessional disorders, is just a stopgap remedy and carries serious side effects.

4 therapy for paroxysmal neurosis

What is Paroxysmal Neurosis?

Paroxysmal neurosis is one of the pathological conditions associated with *shinkeishitsu*. This is a term that I assigned tentatively to various paroxysmal (sudden attack or outburst) symptoms derived from fears that occur in people with *shinkeishitsu*.*

Paroxysmal conditions include palpitation and other painlike attacks. Physicians generally diagnose such conditions as tachycardia, cardiopathy of unknown origin (now called cardiac neurosis), or neurosis subsequent to parturition or disease. Syphilis is sometimes diagnosed on the basis of the Wassermann reaction; physicians adversely keep clients confined to futon and make it almost impossible for them to maintain normal work for years. In my experience, some clients have been mistreated in this way for more than ten years. There is a long-term case of a woman who was married to a restaurant owner. She was restricted by physicians from leaving her home for twenty-two years. Subsequently, she felt uneasy unless either her

---

*Paroxysmal neurosis, as coined by Morita, is similar to the DSM-IV diagnostic category of Acute Stress Disorder.

husband or the restaurant manager were with her in the house.

If clients are physically sound and suffer from attacks of a certain cardiac symptom, they can be cured by just one complete cycle of my method. A twenty-four-year-old male client who worked as a journalist was admitted to our hospital to undergo my therapy for paroxysmal palpitation, a condition that had persisted for about one and one-half years. During initial hospitalization, he had acute diarrhea and an episode of high fever, which returned to normal on his fourth day of treatment. The client decided to endure his attacks and found, subsequently, that his attacks disappeared; he was free of symptoms thirty days after admission. Once a therapist assesses the psychological features of this type of disorder, s/he can easily eliminate the client's symptoms and prevent a recurrence. A few more cases will be presented as illustrations.

A Client with Attacks of Palpitations

A female client who was the wife of a respected university professor and former school teacher of mine, had suffered from attacks of palpitations for four to five years. She reported that the attacks occurred mostly at night. In addition, she was unable to lie down due to anxiety and needed to lean against the bed until the pain disappeared. Once an attack started, it recurred continuously for three to five days. I diagnosed the case as paroxysmal neurosis during our first consultation.

In cases of clients who report attacks of pain, the therapist is advised to determine first if the disorder is organic and, if not, ascertain positively that it is psychogenic in nature. If the actual circumstances of the attacks are unknown, the psychological features of the disorder can be determined by carefully assessing when, where, and how the client's attacks occur. A psychologically-based disorder is often described by the client as an indefinite sensation that is difficult to characterize. The therapist comes to realize that the client's symptoms are produced by the expansion and exaggeration of subjective or objective phenomena associated with the client's fear and astonishment.

On the first day I visited my client, she stated that an attack would occur that very night because she had experienced one the previous night. Taking advantage of this opportunity, I persuaded her to act entirely on my instructions. I told her to assume the lateral position at bedtime (a position in which an attack would be most likely to occur) and to try to induce the attack on her own. I told her to observe carefully the entire course of the attack from the beginning; I promised her that if she did this, I would teach her how to prevent the attacks in the future. I made it known to her that even if she had pain or had to sit up all night, it would be worth enduring this as a means to remove her long-standing pain and anxiety. My client promised to do as I instructed.

On my next visit, the client reported that she had tried to do as I instructed but she could not induce an attack. She fell asleep within five minutes and did not awake until the next morning. When I asked her whether she thought the attacks would occur again, she answered that she believed they would not because she felt completely free from anxiety, though she could not explain the reason. I explained that this was *taitoku* (experiential body understanding)—akin to enlightenment. It is neither theory nor ideology. When she accepted my instruction, she was determined to suffer all night and to plunge into the fear itself. She lost her anxiety about a future attack and was not preoccupied with the idea of escaping it. This is the reason for the attack not occurring. Previously, she had been expecting the attack and had wanted to escape from it; this created mental conflict that further increased her suffering and anxiety. In the future, if she developed similar attacks as a result of convalescence, worry, or overwork, she could eliminate the attacks by consistently facing the situation in a similar manner. This client came to a realization through her experience, without any need for complicated and theoretical explanations from the therapist.

In therapy, just showing the client the point of approach is sufficient. The Zen term *ishin-denshin* (heart speaks to heart) represents this process. When the client tried to induce an attack, s/he was emancipated. Her mental state was similar to that described in the secrets of traditional martial arts by such phrases as *hisshi-hisshō* (being determined to die is being destined to live); *hai-sui-no-jin* (cut off one's own retreat); and *hanmon soku gedatsu* (to be with anguish is to enter the gate of emancipation).

If a person wants to be surprised, s/he cannot be surprised; if one tries to be prepared for death, the proper state of mind for it cannot be obtained. Being surprised or being prepared for death is only possible under certain conditions and circumstances. External circumstances and subjectivity are one and the same at a vital moment. When a person makes assumptions by an ideology and disregards life circumstances, s/he generates the "contradiction by ideas." In the above case, you can easily imagine the result if I had told my client, "If you try to induce the attack, it will never occur and you will be able to sleep well within five minutes. Be sure to try it."

The course described above is not a theory; it is a method that provides clients with practical experience. To regard my method as a kind of suggestive therapy or as *kiai-jutsu* (the technique of controlling another's mind and body by the power of the practitioner's concentrated mind) is not worthy of comment.

A Client with Attacks of Gastrospasm

A sixty-nine-year-old female client had been suffering from gastric pain for ten years. A university department of internal medicine suspected that she had gastric cancer. The following year she was diagnosed as having chilelithiasis by the department of surgery of the same hospital; she did not have surgery despite her physician's advice. Subsequently, the woman visited twelve physicians for treatment without improvement. Finally, Dr. FUTATSUKI diagnosed her case as being neurogenic and referred her to me for a medical examination. Although she was a former acquaintance of mine, I had never thought of carefully inquiring about her symptoms because her disorder appeared to have nothing to do with my specialty. She had a pattern of severe paroxysmal gastric pain that persisted for several months every year. From about one month before my treatment, she had morning and evening attacks that lasted one or two hours twice a day; these sometimes were followed by severe polyuria in the night.

Contrary to my expectation, I found that she did not have actual gastric pain. In most cases, she had a sudden twitching sensation in the right flank that generally occurred at a certain time of day. The pain moved upward and developed into a wringing, burning, and tearing sensation that extended from the gastric region to the inner part of the chest. Upon pain, the client would press her flank tightly with her hand while seated and bend forward; she would then hold her breath, turn pale, and break into cold sweats. This was not gastrospasm in the usual sense, but was similar to the so-called hysterical ball.

Pathologically, I regard this kind of condition as an atypical manifestation of emotional fear caused by psychic interaction. Symptoms of twitching in the flank and intrathoracic tearing can be subjective manifestations of fear. Attack may result from the fear of a possible attack after repeated episodes of actual gastrospasm, or from a particular emotion combined with the fear of gastric pain. Subsequently, by reproducing the spasm pain in one's memory, a client feels as if s/he is in pain. This may resemble an occurrence of centrifugal hallucinations by imagination; the experience is similar to that which occurs in a person who thinks that images in dreams are reality. When attacks occur around the same time of day, they often result from clients' focused attention on their anticipatory fear.

Some scholars attempt to explain the relationship between attention and anticipatory fear by the concept of autosuggestion. I do not agree with the tendency to explain all such mental symptoms by collective terms, such as the subconscience or autosuggestion. It is my belief that the key points of practical treatment cannot be obtained without investigating how the symptoms develop and run a course.

I immediately admitted this client to our hospital and put her into the first isolation-rest phase of treatment. Initially, she had attacks twice a day (morning and evening), one of which occurred around 6:00 P.M. On the first day of therapy, I told her to try to induce a strong attack on her own as much before the expected time of the attack as possible. I informed her that this was necessary for my examination and treatment. However, no attack occurred that evening. During three days of isolation-rest therapy, the client almost produced an attack on a few occasions; yet in spite of her expectation, symptoms soon disappeared. She had a mild attack for the first time on her first day out of bed. On this occasion she had engaged in talking, a behavior that is prohibited during this stage of treatment.

In response to her attack, I quickly and forcefully pressed both sides of her neck at the seventh cervical vertebra with my fingers. The client felt a strong pain, but the attack disappeared as soon as a swelling-up feeling in her chest diminished. Thereafter, she underwent the successive work therapy for about ten days. Following my therapy, she had no further attacks and was discharged with complete recovery. Two years later, this client had an episode of hemoptysis but soon recovered; she has been well without recurrence of pain for the past seven years.

A Client with Attacks Resembling Labor Pain

A thirty-one-year-old woman of primigravida was admitted to a maternity hospital for an attack of laborlike pain

more than one month before the expected date of her delivery. There was no sign of the onset of labor despite the
injection of a labor-inducing drug. Injection of analgesics
also produced no effect. The woman was placed in bed by
a physician for sixteen days after admission, at which time
she claimed she was unable to sit on the bed.

I knew this woman's history because I had previously
treated her for fear of fainting. She had symptoms of
shinkeishitsu with former complaints of palpitation and vertigo. Given our previous association, her husband consulted
me about referring her to a gynecologist. Before making
such arrangements, I visited her and found, contrary to my
expectation, that her pain was psychogenic.

Her paroxysmal pain developed first at the left flank
and then shifted to the right. It became broad ranging and
was induced by almost any physical movement; she finally
forced herself to lie immobile on her back. The initial attacks
lasted for several minutes; over time, they progressed to a
couple of hours until they became continuous.

Her pain was not inflammatory or spastic and was of
an indescribable nature accompanied by twitching and a
heavy feeling. The woman had a previous history of tuber-
culous diathesis with pleurisy. A few years earlier, a nut-
sized induration was palpable at the caecal area following
infiltration in the pulmonary apex. More recently, she had
received prolonged gynecological treatment for ovaritis. Although many organic disorders were previously diagnosed,
I assessed the case as psychogenic on the basis of palpitation at the site of pain, and observation of patterns of change
in the site and development of the attack.

During my first visit, the woman had little pain for
about two hours. In an attempt to make her induce an attack on her own, I ordered her to assume a lateral position
with her right side down, the position in which the attack
was reported to have always occurred. Following several
attempts, no attack occurred. Then I told her to sit on the
bed and to leave the bedside and walk around the room.
The result was the same. During our two-hour session, the

client failed to induce an attack. In this way, the woman became confident that the attacks would not recur. (This paradoxical result has occurred in other clients I have treated.)

Two days later, on my second visit, I was confident that the attacks were gone and arranged for her to leave the hospital. Although the client almost had a mild attack on a few occasions, she was no longer concerned and had a normal delivery about one month later.

My therapy for those assessed with paroxysmal neurosis (acute stress disorder) is simple and does not require medical intervention; yet it is fundamental as treatment. Therapists may not believe this until they actually observe the results of this method of intervention. Most importantly, this therapy requires an accurate diagnosis. If the diagnosis is correct, the methods of therapy become clear. Psychotherapy performed by nonprofessionals may sometimes bring miraculous recoveries. However, it must be kept in mind that therapy can harm a client if assessment and diagnosis are ignored.

5   therapy for obsessive disorders and phobias

Nature of Obsessive Disorders

There are distinguishing points between those diagnosed with obsessive disorders and those with ordinary *shinkeishitsu*. Clients with ordinary *shinkeishitsu* tend to report symptoms of physical pain, fear, habitual heavy feelings in the head, vertigo, and insomnia. Those with obsessive disorders generate complicated inner conflicts; for example, they feel ashamed of themselves for feeling shy or embarrassed, or they try not to feel pain in spite of the fact that the pain is being experienced. In the same way, they try not to feel fear of their fear of tuberculosis to such an extent that they develop anticipatory fear of what they fear.

A key point regarding obsessive disorders is that the thought patterns represent an exaggeration of tendencies any person could have; the thought patterns are not part of a serious disease. Consider the case of a person who became anxious about the tip of his nose. Each person has the ability to see the tip of her or his nose when looking down to read a book. Yet, one is usually not aware of the nose because "the eye is blind if the mind is absent." The development of an obsessive disorder depends on whether a person ignores the nose or fixates on it. Inner conflicts occur between acknowledging the tip of the nose as it naturally exists and resisting its presence; this develops further into mental preoccupation and obsessive thinking (see Editor's Glossary of Morita Therapy Terms).

The following examples illustrate how a minor event can initiate obsessive disorders. A man with a beautiful beard in ancient China became preoccupied with his beard after the king asked him what he did with his beard when he went to sleep. A student feared for the tip of her or his nose after seeing it for the first time while studying for examinations. Another person developed a fear for trembling because s/he noticed trembling hands during the exchange of the nuptial cups. A man developed a fear of profanity and uncleanness after becoming concerned about the dirtiness of his hands while making an offering to the family's Buddhist alter.

Although the development and progression of ordinary *shinkeishitsu* is different from an obsessive disorder, there are many cases that fall somewhere in the middle. For example, anxiety about facing a particular situation can develop from obsessive thinking. In some cases, this is manifested by the disorder I have called "paroxysmal neurosis." Clients may have attacks of palpitations, vertigo, or a feeling of syncope when in certain situations, such as in a crowd of people, in a solitary place, on a train, on the street, or in a physician's examination room. *Shinkeishitsu* is manifested in those who believe that they are ill and actually have an attack, while those with obsessive disorders realize that they are not actually ill but have anticipatory fears of the attack.

Therapeutic Focus in Treating Obsessive Disorders

When treating clients with obsessive disorders, I focus initial treatment on eliminating clients' complex inner conflicts and restoring their pain or fear to a simple state. Treatment involves instilling certain psychological attitudes in clients, such as telling them to persevere with their condition as it is (without denying or avoiding their pain or fear), instructing them not to direct their minds away from discomfort, and showing them how to practice these attitudes. This is indeed contrary to prescriptions by DuBois (1908) and others, who tell clients to "Overcome it!"; "Eliminate pain from your mind!"; "Don't let such an idea into your mind!"; or "Keep a big mind!" Directing or forcing clients in this manner will only distress them and create even more complicated inner conflicts for them. This kind of approach is like adding fuel to a fire. The psychological features of an obsessive disorder are a preexisting condition, and symptoms are exacerbated when clients are directed to overcome them. During an event or experience, a person has the ability to refrain from acting out an impulse. However, it is impossible not to have some feelings or thoughts associated with the event or impulse. A person cannot avoid feeling anger when someone speaks ill of him or her; yet s/he can refrain from quarreling over the matter. There is a saying by Confucius (952–479 B.C.): "Acknowledging what we do not know is to know it." I would say, "Thinking that something impossible is possible is the mark of a fool."

Those with obsessive disorders are in danger of interpreting citations as narrow passages and of making superficial interpretations. For example, the Bible states, "He who looks at a woman with lust has already committed adultery in his mind. If your right eye offends you, pluck it out and cast it away." This passage represents an idealistic viewpoint that requires a person to do the impossible and deny her or his actual emotions. This represents the contradiction by ideas that I have discussed. If one interprets a Bible quotation literally without considering extended explanations, one might begin to develop obsessive thoughts and focus on the fear of morality. When Socrates was told by a physiognomist that he had the seal of lewdness on his face, he said that this was true and that he had controlled part of his nature. This is a pragmatic and practical response based on facts. KURATA Momozō wrote about a series of his experiences of suffering from obsessive ideas during his artistic contemplation in the magazine *Seikatsu-sha* ("Absolute Living," 1891–1943). His writing shows clearly how his obsessive thinking resulted from his idealistic thinking.

Plunge into Fear

Clients with obsessive ideas of the simple type who have clear understanding or insight and who try suggestions offered by the therapist can sometimes be cured by persuasion therapy (as described in the previous section). The cure is achieved when the client plunges into her or his fear (as shown in the above-mentioned case of paroxysmal neurosis). For example, a therapist may tell a client who cannot board a train because of the fear of blushing, "Gather your courage, get on a train, and show your bursting red face to all the people." This urges the client to take action immediately. One such client overcame a persistent fear of blushing within only three or four days after persuasion. In a way, this method creates a psychological condition similar to that produced by confession. A person can become free from the fixated focus on ego defenses by making an open confession about her or himself in public.

Clients with an obsessive disorder think incorrectly that any attempt to resist or endure their fear will intensify the fear and aggravate their inner conflict; hence, they suffer from anticipatory fear. Accordingly, they cannot plunge into their fear alone. The plunge is only possible when they are supported, encouraged, and directed by a therapist who has a strong sense of conviction. Clients who delve too far into theory or are too skeptical or noncompliant are unable to take the plunge. Once the plunge into fear has been taken, the client has burned the bridges and is able to experience egolessness; in this way s/he comprehends an absolute obedience to nature. The more complicated types of obsessive disorders are difficult to eliminate. It is noted that if the therapist's instructions fail to produce the expected results, the client may suffer a psychological setback.

In most cases the best choice of treatment is my special four-stage therapy for ordinary *shinkeishitsu*. Up to the end of stage three, it is recommended that work therapy be performed according to the general rules and that clients are not told about the recovery process for obsessive disorders or the psychological attitude required for its cure.

Additional mental training is necessary if the client has poor attention, faulty thinking, or an active imagination. Treatment for those with obsessive disorders is undertaken during stage four and the therapist directs the client to plunge into his or her fear. For example, a client with a fear of fire would be given work related to fire.

Recovery in a Client with a Fear of Stealing

A twenty-four-year-old woman who worked on a farm developed a phobia five years prior to treatment. Her major symptom, a fear of stealing from other people, had no particular motivation and was accompanied by other obsessive ideas, such as the fear of uncleanness, fire, and portents. She had restricted the movement of her body for six months. She just lay on her back because she feared that her hands might steal something without her being aware of it. In addition, she feared that if she ate food that was cooked, a flame would spew from her mouth and start a fire. Having been in bed for nearly one year, the client developed a critical condition.

Within two months after admission, I treated this woman and achieved a complete recovery from this complicated and severe obsessive and phobic disorder. A possible precursor to this case was the fact that five years earlier, the client had exchanged a kimono for a new one because the initial purchase did not satisfy her. Since then, she had not been able to touch the kimono; she kept it hidden away in a drawer because of her fear that she had obtained it by dishonest methods similar to shoplifting.

One night, about one month after her admission, I told my client to put on the kimono, which I had brought from her home, and I instructed her to go to bed wearing it. I told her to be prepared to suffer all night. Unexpectedly, she fell asleep easily, and slept through the night. The next morning she thanked me for enabling her to experience the mental condition that had resulted from plunging into her fear.

In another experiment with the same client, I told her before bedtime to try to obtain the most comfortable sleeping position by carefully studying the conditions under which she would be able to sleep best, including her posture, position of the arms and legs, and the placement of her head on the pillow. During the night she suffered greatly and was unable to sleep well. The next night, I told her to maintain her initial position in bed without trying to change it. I said to stay in the same position and remain awake all night no matter how uncomfortable the initial position might be. The next morning this client came to me beaming with delight and reported that she had slept soundly. Through experience, she was able to understand the mental state required to be able to sleep. The above episode indicates that clients' expectations or thoughts may be completely opposite to reality. This condition is known as the "contradiction by ideas."

In clients such as those presented above, therapy begins with treatment of the least threatening obsessive thoughts; when appropriate, therapy proceeds to plunge them into the fear from which they suffer most intensely. Once they experience the state of mind that results from plunging into fear, other manifestations of obsessive ideas spontaneously disappear. Those clients who find that they accomplish what they had previously been unable to do— simply by adopting a firm and decisive manner—become delighted with their successive accomplishments and gradually feel more courageous. Those with obsessive thinking who are deficient in feelings of delight and appreciation are more difficult to cure, and those with certain personality disorders (or weak-willed characters) are usually unable to feel delight.

Course of Treatment

In rare cases, clients gain an understanding that their obsessive ideas are an illusion. Sometimes, they respond as if they attained spiritual enlightenment. Consider the case of a twenty-four-year-old man who had not been able to read or count for a few years because he had fears of reading and calculation. On the twenty-first day after admission to our hospital, in stage three of my therapy, the client obtained a sudden flash of understanding when lifting an ax to chop wood. He light-heartedly returned to his room to review and record his mental condition at the time. During contemplation and diary writing, he found that his condition was entirely consistent with what I had told him by means of persuasion. Following this insight, he was discharged without evidence of obsessive thinking or fears of calculations and reading. This episode helps to show that if clients begin with theory and force their minds to fit the theory, then contradiction by ideas and "incorrect" ideation results. In contrast, by beginning with one's own actual experience, or what I call the "pure mind," an eventual correct description and review of the condition lead to "correct" ideation. Things that cannot be understood with "incorrect" ideation are easily and quickly known with "correct" ideation.

I disagree with the theory that phenomena are explained, not by natural science, but by teleology. From a teleological viewpoint, all the plants and animals on earth have been created for humans. When discussed from the viewpoint of natural science, first there was the land, and then living organisms appeared on that land. Humans survive only because plants and animals became available as food. Contrary to Freud's theory (1896b, 1900), dreams and hysteria are not caused by desire, but occur in the course of various psychological conditions, including desire. It must be determined whether Freudian theory comprises "incorrect" ideation or "correct" ideation. This issue needs further study in the future.

The twenty-year-old client, described previously as having a fear of immorality, gained understanding of his "correct" state of mind while shoveling feces. In general, clients will gradually acquire self-confidence and courage. But cure without recurrence can be achieved only after experiencing, at least once, the mental state of plunging into the fear.

According to usual descriptions given by clients, their experience after being cured is like "awakening from a dream," or a "dawning in an understanding," or feeling "as if the world has changed." In recalling their previous condition, some clients feel as if it were a dream, others state that they cannot understand how they could have had such obsessive ideas. When clients attain this stage, they correctly understand the common saying, "positive or negative judgments, as long as they are made in a dream, are unreliable and are akin to those made while in a state of mental confusion." *Sandōkai* (one of the Zen classics) states, "If we walk without knowing the way, merely going forward will not yield the right path. Distance does not matter. What matters is the right path; going astray leads one far away from the right path." *Satori* (enlightenment) and "correct" ideation are obtained by experientially knowing the reality of daily life that is right before one's eyes. Once trapped in contradiction by ideas, one cannot escape confusion, even if s/he believes she has attained enlightenment or resolved the problem. Treatment developed by DuBois (1908), which tries to make clients overcome their fear or develop self-confidence by logical persuasion, inevitably results in the recurrence of the client's initial problem, even though clients may temporarily seem improved.

Some clients with ordinary *shinkeishitsu* or an obsessive or phobic disorder who achieved complete recovery during inpatient therapy, become anxious about whether they can lead an active, confident life at home. If this happens, clients are encouraged to cope with the circumstance at hand and experience their anxiety, without clinging to their self-confidence and courage. In essence, it is "incorrect" ideation to live with a false peace of mind fabricated by one's own ideas and assumptions that the world is an unchanging refuge for oneself. One can find true peace of mind only when one accepts the fact that human life is transient and unstable.

In actuality, it is not possible for my clients to imagine what their home will be like after discharge because their image is based on the memory of their experience before therapy and recovery. They cannot know the situation until they actually are in it. In fact, clients are sometimes surprised by the changes they encounter after going home. A family that once felt cold, now feels congenial in atmosphere; a spouse or partner who may have seemed harsh is now seen as kind; and classmates who may have appeared hostile now seem frank. It is not the circumstances but the clients themselves who have changed. A client's former anxiety may have been created by a situation like that of a person who imagines her or his face when no mirror exists. Indeed, following my therapy, clients see themselves reflected in the mirror of the minds of those around them for the first time. This reminds me of a verse, "When we look at mountains with a smile, the mountains smile back; when we look at water through our tears, the water also cries."

6   persuasion therapy

What is Persuasion Therapy?

Persuasion therapy uses logical persuasion to treat clients who have anxiety or delusion-based symptoms in order to decrease their false or incorrect ideation. From earliest times across cultures, therapists have had various therapeutic techniques for treating those with delusions and anxiety disorders. These methods, however, are based on a framework of common sense and don't attend to the pathology that drives symptoms.

    In ancient China, a client who feared uncleanness was influenced by the following persuasion: "Since cereals are all derived from soil mixed with excrement, and well water is mixed with the excretions of insects, your particular fear of uncleanness holds no ground." Rosenbach performed gastric irrigation on a client with hypochondriasis who was convinced of having gastric cancer; he claimed that he cured his client by the following persuasion, "Now, following this treatment, you are not different from a healthy person." However, if Rosenbach's client had been delusional or obsessional in her or his thinking, such a positive outcome would not have occurred. In fact, if a cure had been achieved, the client might only have been liberated from an anticipatory anxiety which s/he would have created by her or his own misunderstanding.

Clients with *shinkeishitsu* generally become hypochondriac after they experience a certain sensation or event. Subsequently, they develop symptoms and obsessive ideas on the basis of their emotions, such as anticipatory worry, fear, or anxiety associated with their faulty thinking. Emotions form the original base from which subsequent ideas are generated. Therefore, the initial treatment for clients with obsessive disorders requires a focus on their emotional base. Similarly, although the voluntary muscles are under our direct control according to our desires and thoughts, smooth muscles and emotions are not under our direct control.

Adverse Effects of Logical Persuasion

A thirty-five-year-old woman developed hypochondriasis with a fear of germs and uncleanness after being suspected of having pulmonary tuberculosis. Naturally, most people are upset or worried when a physician suspects they have pulmonary tuberculosis or cancer. Only a child or person with psychosis would not be upset in this situation. However, not all clients with pulmonary tuberculosis or cancer develop obsessive thoughts. Normal people are concerned with their physical health and have no conflicts caused by complex ideation. The normal condition is comparable to that of a child who cries loudly when in grief but soon becomes cheerful. In contrast, clients with obsessive disorders believe that their fear and mental anguish are incomparably painful and a sign of their pathological suffering. They envy others and grieve over their own misfortune; consequently, they cause more conflicts and aggravate their symptoms by attempting to deny, eliminate, or overcome the suffering.

If a physician or therapist attempts to persuade such a client that s/he does not have pulmonary tuberculosis or cancer without attending to the client's underlying primary base of emotions, then the professional's efforts will align with the client's psychopathology and intensify the client's fears. This is like adding fuel to a fire because the therapist's neglect causes the client's fearful emotions to become much stronger. When clients attempt to eliminate their fears of disease and attain peace of mind, they maintain a state of tense mind that leads them to feel deeper disappointment and pessimism. This is comparable to the phenomenon that the more people earnestly attempt to pursue comfort and pleasure, the more they fall into the state of disappointment and pessimism; they believe strongly that all their desires are not fulfilled. When a client actually recognizes pulmonary tuberculosis, the obsessive ideas associated with the fear of it are not present. In this case, the client with *shinkeishitsu* might manifest fear of insomnia or loss of appetite and develop an obsessive disorder related to the potential dangers associated with the cure for tuberculosis. These fears are different from the fear of tuberculosis itself.

When persuasion therapy attempts to show clients that they do not have gastric cancer or pulmonary tuberculosis, clients understand by their intellect and logic that they do not have the disease and they feel relief from anxiety. Yet, it is naive to think that as a result of reduced anxiety, hypochondriasis has been improved and obsessive ideas have disappeared. The focus of clients' obsessive ideas will simply shift to another area, while their hypochondriacal tendencies will result in fears of other physical or mental sensations. As fear is continually stimulated by clients' hypochondriacal tendencies, they further intensify their preoccupation with illness by becoming attached to the fear. Therefore, unless clients are discharged from their basic emotions that drive their hypochondriacal tendencies, their anxiety will never abate itself.

Although clients may be temporarily relieved from anxiety about a specific disease like cancer or tuberculosis, they will continue to harbor a fear that they will be taken seriously ill, at any moment, in this unstable life. They fear they have a latent disease that physicians cannot find, or they think they have a pathogenic bacteria that will suddenly harm them. Preoccupied with such suspicions, they develop endless cycles of doubts and new fears of disease, germs, or uncleanness; they may worry about passing or transmitting the disease to their family and children.

In order to break down these feelings of fear and anxiety, it is essential that clients first become obedient to the uncertainty of human life as it is. Through correct ideation they realize that people are open to disease at any time because the human body is porous and susceptible to illness. Therapy can assist them to endure their fear of disease, no matter how great it is, and to do what is required in daily living to assist their goals of life. In other words, they are directed to rid themselves of the contradiction by ideas, accept and endure the reality of their feelings as they are (without denying feelings), and to stop endeavors or manipulations to suppress or remove these feelings.

In the case of the above-mentioned woman, her physicians made extreme efforts to prove to her that she was not ill; they developed X-ray films in her presence to show her that no tuberculosis lesions existed, and they compared these films with those of infected people. As a result, her obsessive thinking emerged in another area. I assessed this woman and diagnosed *shinkeishitsu* with obsessive thinking. I treated her with my four-stage therapy. Initially she cried and endured her pain; following the course of therapy, she achieved a complete recovery.

Attachment to Ego

Before applying persuasion therapy, I encourage therapists to assess the degree to which clients have an understanding of their direct experiences that are not self-focused. When clients are governed by symptoms, they confine and attach themselves to their ego. They are unable to view or understand things outside their attachment to ego-centered desires. This process is comparable to a person being unable to judge whether something is right or wrong while dreaming. For example, the female client with the fear of pulmonary tuberculosis said, "I would rather have Hansen's disease than suffer anxiety like this." Although this client would have had far greater pessimism and anguish if she actually had Hansen's disease (leprosy), it was impossible to make her understand this fact. When I tried to persuade her by pointing to the fact that she had gained four pounds in a short period of time, she answered, "Nutrition doesn't matter to me when I am suffering this anguish." She could not understand that nutrition was integral to her health when she was "self" focused and demanding.

I will quote a couple of cases that use persuasion therapy with clients who have ordinary *shinkeishitsu*. In response to a physician's assessment that no disease could be found, ordinary *shinkeishitsu* clients often say, "But I must be ill because my usually cheerful disposition has suddenly changed"; "I am nervous about trifles and feel melancholy"; or "I must have some disease because I feel a strong pulse all over my body and an intense beating in my heart, whereas I didn't have this feeling before." The therapist can offer the following explanation to such clients: "These feelings are not new ones and they have not been caused by an organic disorder, such as inflammation or metabolic disease. On some previous occasion you became aware of something that existed but took no notice and ignored it. Recently, you became preoccupied with it because of your increasing concern about it. You are not actually ill."

To make it clearer, a few more examples are given. Some years ago, a thirty-year-old woman happened to feel her heart beating when she touched her chest as she lay in bed. She was surprised by this sensation and rushed to a physician with the complaint that something alive was inside her chest. This woman had not been aware of the presence of her heart until the age of thirty. Another example is that of the previously mentioned Chinese man with the long beard. He could not sleep after he became self-conscious of his beard and soon developed an increasing concern about its presence. Also, clients who fear the tip of their nose are unaware of its continual presence until after they focus attention on it. Such cases are common. Those who are not observant do not realize that they could have seen the tip of their own nose since birth. There are a number of people who claim that they have never had a dream because they make claim to the common saying, "Saints do not dream." However, this passage does not mean literally that saints do not dream. If a person pauses to reflect immediately upon awakening, it is clear that s/he has had a dream. Those with *shinkeishitsu* complain of having too many dreams because they are very preoccupied with their dreams, while ordinary people say they have few dreams because they are not concerned with the frequency of their dreams. The so-called saints who direct themselves to have no dreams are actually those who lack an introspective mind.

Ego-Centered Dogmatism

Most clients with *shinkeishitsu* constantly complain, "I alone suffer while others are highly spirited and enjoy life." We persuade them by asking, "By what kind of standard and observation do you compare yourself against others? How have you decided that you alone suffer, or feel cold or hot? Does this experience come from an indulgence in self?" Few clients, however, digest and understand this kind of intervention. Only a well-disciplined mind can appreciate the meaning of self in this regard. Educated people may understand how the earth looks when viewed from the moon, but it is difficult for them to see their own mind from the viewpoint of someone else.

Furthermore, some *shinkeishitsu* clients are continually disappointed because they think no one understands them or sympathizes with them. These clients do not answer in a positive way when asked, "Do you want other people to know everything about your innermost feelings?" They want others to understand only those aspects that could be advantageous to themselves, not those that would disadvantage them. In short, these clients are self-serving. Their intention is to make their unfavorable circumstances known to others by confession or self-disclosure. They realize that when they confess a difficulty, others act empathically toward them; and if they present only favorable events, they receive little attention or sympathy. The old word *chiki* (rendered as one's friend, or one who fully understands) is a relationship made possible only in a highly developed person. During hospitalization, when clients with *shinkeishitsu* are forbidden to complain about their conditions, they begin to gain experiential understanding while decreasing their need for intellectual understanding.

Attachment as a Biased View

Obsessive disorders usually develop from attachment. Attachment occurs when a person views only one aspect of something with the mind fixated and ignores the panorama. For example, the mind becomes attached when one believes life is all suffering; s/he loses sight of the fact that life is alternately bitter and sweet. Efforts and worries are prerequisites for the fulfillment of human desire. For instance, people worry about obtaining a certain occupational position or having enough money. The greater the desire, the greater the worry. Clients with obsessive disorders try to deny their suffering without abandoning their desire; they become preoccupied with the pain that accompanies their efforts and disregard the pleasures of fulfilling their desire. For example, obsessive ideas that accompany a fear of reading books is frequently found in people who make excellent marks in school. It is a contradiction when clients achieve good results in spite of their conviction that they cannot read. Such clients are not satisfied with their results. However, most books contain both easy and difficult parts and a person naturally comprehends what is understandable and misses the parts that are beyond her or his ability. That is to say, one becomes pleased at what one understands and makes laborious efforts on the difficult parts.

Clients who have a fear of reading claim that they cannot understand everything in a book; they become attached to a perfect method of reading and preoccupied with worry. This attachment, however, dissolves when they undergo the prescribed reading program used in my hospitalization therapy. Following several days of treatment, they are able to read freely, regardless of time and place.

The onset of mental attachment and preoccupation is induced by unavoidable circumstances, and the contradiction by ideas is caused by attempts not to be preoccupied. In order to rid oneself of this contradiction, it is necessary to simply comply with the original mental preoccupation. Once there is a natural flow of the mind, attachments will diminish spontaneously as one's mind changes in response to stimuli from the external world. There is a saying, "The human mind changes with the environment in the most subtle and profound ways. Realization of the nature of the mind according to its natural flow enables a person to surpass both joy and sorrow." The mind is always changing as circumstances change. Like a bell that is loud when struck forcefully and soft when tolled gently, the smooth, free, and flexible changing flow of our mind is both extremely subtle and profound. The mind is like a mirror; things are reflected when they come in front of it and disappear when they pass by it. Through obedience to the flow of the mind, one can find primary human nature. In this situation, joy is just joy and sorrow is just sorrow. It is not necessary to worry about worry intentionally, and it is not possible to worry when one is full of joy. Joy and sorrow cannot be intentionally manipulated by one's intellect. Clients are directed to abandon their analytical approach to joy and sorrow, change their feeling-centered "attitudes" to a fact-centered stance (which maintains that emotions are facts not to be denied), and take the facts—as they are.

Attitude toward Fear

With respect to the mental attitude toward fear, there is a proverb, "The hounds of desire return each time they are driven away." The object of a person's obsessive thinking is like a dog barking at a person. The barking dog will lunge at a person's leg the instant an intent to flee is shown. Even if the person breaks into a run, human speed can be no match for a running dog. In contrast, if a person holds a dog's gaze and moves closer, then the dog will hold back. It is said that the charm that wards off a dog bite is the action of writing the word *tiger* with a finger on the palm of one's hand three times, and standing up with the hand closed tightly. This simply suggests that one is advised to stay still and appear calm. The object of a person's obsessive thoughts is not as dangerous as a live dog. As in the case of an Acute Anxiety Disorder, if one adopts an attitude of facing the object without averting the eyes, it will enable one to ascertain the object's nature. This is described in the saying, "The ghost feared at night is actually a withered pampas grass in the daylight."

Religious and Philosophical Persuasion

Caution is advised when philosophical or religious persuasion appeals to the intellect and is not practical. From the viewpoint of natural science, God is not an actual entity; rather, God is a transitional psychological object that is created by different cultural groups. What a person calls God, Buddha, or the Absolute is actually the truth of the universe, that is, the law of nature itself. True religion is not something that exists to gratify human desires, to cure an illness, or obtain peace of mind and a life of ease. The best approach to Buddha or God is to remain obedient to the laws of nature, to accept the nature of causality, and to accept and appreciate one's own and another person's situation. The circulation of blood in the human body, the experience of emotion, and associated thoughts are all expressions of the true nature of all things in the universe and are governed by natural law. Dreams, ideas, forgetfulness, and mental preoccupations all have their origins. Headache and vertigo are included in Amitabha's dispensation: "The human experiences of anguish and fear are also governed by natural law and inevitably occur."

As humans, we cannot overcome natural law, we can simply obey it and accept the fact that the impossible is impossible. This is true faith. In contrast, when we try to make the impossible possible, when we deceive or make excuses for ourselves, or when we comfort ourselves and assume a false feeling of security at hand, we are participating in superstition. It is truthful to accept the heavy feeling in our head that comes from rising late or the feeling of discomfort that comes from overeating. Superstition is present in those who believe a pear is an omen for making money because of the sound of its name; when a pear is called *ari-no-mi* instead of *nashi* (the original name for pear in Japanese), it means "having possessions." Superstition is present in those who overeat and take digestives after every meal, or in those at a shrine or a temple who try to make money on the stock market by offering a bit of money to a deity.

Some of my clients have been dogmatic followers of various religions, such as Tenriism, the Kurozumi Sect, Christianity, the Shinshu Sect of Buddhism. After experiencing obedience to nature as taught by my therapy, many of these followers recognize that their previous approach to faith is false and they have came to understand true faith for the first time. For example, some clients who attempt to find a cure for their disorder with the help of the religious leader, Reverend KUROZUMI, feel more justified in their own suffering when they realize that their leader also suffers too.

Therapists are encouraged to use persuasion therapy cautiously; they are to consider the client's life circumstances and individual knowledge as it exists, as well as the client's level of practical experience. Needless to say, it is important that therapists give strong and patient encouragement that is grounded in a firm view of life (and nature) when treating their clients.

Furthermore, therapists are obligated to make a precise and accurate diagnosis of their clients. It is vital that they understand the psychological condition of their clients prior to administering persuasion therapy. Obsessive disorders can be mistaken as a catalyst to a compulsive act or a delusion; these disorders may be misdiagnosed as the early stage of a hebephrenic type of schizophrenia. A compulsive act comes out of a congenital disorder or a personality disorder. In contrast, delusion is an acquired condition that involves a state of apathy. When clients with the above disorders are subjected to the same kind of persuasion therapy that is applied to those with obsessive disorders, persuasion will not only fail to improve their mental state but may cause adverse reactions.

Return to Nature

Since the suffering of which clients complain has been aggravated by their initial misdirected mental attitude, it disappears immediately if they return to the human natural condition. Nature mimics and signifies the reality of human life. When clients view human life as it is and recognize that human life is painful to other people and themselves, they will be able to accept the occurrence of suffering, fear, and delight. Shakamuni Buddha's great enlightenment was not attained by experiencing human life as comfortable. The Buddha attained spiritual enlightenment and peace of mind by realizing some of the most difficult facts of life: nothing is permanent, all things pass away, and all living things die.

Sandōkai says, "When each nature of the four cosmic elements—earth, water, fire, and wind—returns to normal, it is like a child who finds a mother: fire is hot, wind blows, water is cool, and earth is firm." Delusion develops in a person who wants to feel coolness from a fire or warmth from water. When restored to the natural condition, one feels cold in winter, fears disease, dislikes uncleanliness, and sometimes feels shy in front of others. Obsessive disorders are driven by a person's voracity and desires, such as wanting to feel warm in winter or cool in summer. Desire does not exist if one returns to the origins of human nature. For example, the fear of blushing develops when a person harbors an inappropriate desire to act more boldly in public than others. Frequent complaints by clients with *shinkeishitsu* (such as, "Life doesn't seem worth living") result from an excessive desire for immortality. Clients who say that they want to die rather than suffer the fear of disease or germs have a contradiction by ideas that originates from their fear of death; sometimes, they are in a desperate and wayward childlike state. When a person is truly prepared for death, fear disappears immediately.

7 experiential therapy for the treatment of anxiety-based disorders

Relation to Other Disorders

The fear of death and disease is part of human nature. The psychic interaction generated by these fears also represents a natural psychological process in humans. Though these fears are common to all people, they tend to be overly activated in individuals inclined to *shinkeishitsu*. In this way, no person is completely free from the *shinkeishitsu* process.

Therefore, it is not true that the treatment of *shinkeishitsu* has no relation with other diseases. Clients with valvular heart disease, diabetes, pulmonary tuberculosis, neuralgia, myelopathy, or even apoplectic hemiplegia occasionally have prominent *shinkeishitsu* symptoms. Most of these disorders can be successfully treated. Clients with diabetes and valvular heart disease will be able to live a healthier life when they acquire the proper mental attitude toward their illness, practice correct daily habits, and engage in spontaneous healthy activities. Complete cures have been reported by clients with hemiplegia who were treated by nonmedical therapists with *kiai-jutsu*. Reported recoveries from chronic disease through other forms of treatment indicate that the symptoms in these clients coincided with *shinkeishitsu* symptoms; thus, the effectiveness of alternative methods occurs by accident and not by methods based on the formal diagnosis of *shinkeishitsu*.

Sensitivity to Symptoms

When a person is psychologically healthy, s/he is aware of endogenous and exogenous stimulation, and does not over or under estimate the stimulation. One's recognition of abnormal sensations that accompany disorders is called "sensitivity to symptoms," while recognition or understanding of the fact that one is afflicted with a disorder is termed "awareness of disease."

When the range of sensations or emotions that naturally occur across humans become exaggerated, or when someone's symptoms are felt very intensely, that person is said to be hypersensitive to their own symptoms. Those with *shinkeishitsu* are continually hypersensitive to their subjective symptoms. In contrast, those with schizophrenia or some personality disorders are not especially aware of pain; in many cases, they show decreased sensitivity to symptoms even when they are actually ill. Sometimes children are not aware of having a high fever when they are lost in play. Occasionally we hear about a sudden death by cardiac arrest or beriberi in a young person who just graduated from high school. Such a person must have become over stressed prior to the onset of the physical crisis because s/he had not been sufficiently aware of her or his own symptoms. Hence, cardiac disease of the acute type does not seem to lead to this *shinkeishitsu*-like sudden critical episode. In contrast, those inclined to *shinkeishitsu* are convinced that they feel abnormalities, such as frequent palpitation, even without a diagnosis of disorder.

Therefore, the actual severity of a disorder does not always coincide with or run parallel to the sufferer's awareness of symptoms. Some fatal illnesses carry no subjective symptoms, while others are not a matter for alarm regardless of severe suffering. When physicians and therapists regard only subjective symptoms as important in treating an illness, they may be concerning themselves with minor details and neglecting fundamental points. When assessing *shinkeishitsu*, it is irresponsible to determine the severity of the disorder only on the basis of the clients' complaints since the subjective complaints are often misleading. In fact, most physicians will misdiagnose *shinkeishitsu* as severe neurasthenia when the client reports severe suffering, and mild neurasthenia when the client reports mild suffering. Physicians often administer sedatives to clients who complain of insomnia without bothering to learn the fact that the client lies in bed for twelve hours indulging in sleep, or the client is leading an unhealthy schedule in daily life. In response to the client's complaint of headaches, some physicians readily give analgesics and prescribe rest, without asking about the relation between the headaches and the client's lifestyle. If a physician had true compassion for the sick, s/he would refrain from such practice.

Religion and View of Life

People develop overwhelming fears associated with the four inevitable events in human life: suffering, aging, becoming ill, and dying. The origins of most religions have been based on recognizing and responding to these events. When a person transcends her or his ego and refrains from satisfying egocentric desires with religion, s/he can find liberation, peace of mind, and the meaning of true religion. It is only in this regard that true human nature and the treatment of *shinkeishitsu* are related with religion.

In the treatment of *shinkeishitsu*, clients are discouraged from becoming attached to and preoccupied with their thoughts, depending on their subjective ideals, or behaving to satisfy their emotions and infatuations. Treatment is designed to stress the importance of reality; practical facts are to be experienced through spontaneous activities of the mind=body. That is, therapy is not based on those principles that encourage momentary happiness or superficial pleasure; rather therapy is conducted on the basis of the principles that highlight practice. In this way, clients will experientially understand that to make an effort is to move towards true contentment; true happiness is achieved by making an effort. This presents a more accurate view of life.

The mental training to which I speak is not based on theory or philosophy, nor does it concern the contradiction by ideas generated by those who advocate idealism and moralism. My therapy is different from Zen, which prescribes sitting in meditation. It is "training by experiencing practical events," as described by O-YO-MEI (MING Wang Yang: 1472–1528). My training does not direct a person to concentrate her or his mental energy solely on the hypogastric region, as practiced in the art of abdominal yogic breathing. Misdirected people tend to seek mental training in some kind of theory, or they try to force themselves to fit into a certain categorical framework. This process is like making an initial error of an inch and ending up a thousand miles off the right course. Be careful not to make such mistakes by the contradiction of ideas. Rather, my methods concentrate on simple and routine work, such as carrying buckets of water and chopping wood, from which a person learns to respond to changes in the environment.

The Relationship between Superstition and Obsessive Disorders

Superstition and religion are like twins; they sprout from the same seed; one becomes a maze of branches, while the other becomes a road to spiritual enlightenment. Superstition is self-deception; deception occurs when one does not face the four inevitable events in human life (suffering, aging, becoming ill, and dying); whereas, true faith represents the transcendence of ego. (Obsessive disorders associated with the fear of profanity or portents are examples of how superstition develops.)

The founder of Tenriism had a child with rheumatalgia, and the founder of Konkō-kyō had peritonsillitis. When they received an ascetic form of faith healing for these diseases, both of them were inspired and their personalities were transformed. Their religions sprouted from these events. Tenriism, in particular, has a direct link to the treatment of disease and developed through a course similar to Christian Science in the United States. They both refer to themselves as therapeutic religions. Accordingly, many of the followers of these religions embraced faith when cured of their disease. Some, for example, were cured of headache by drinking water given by a religious leader. However, I wonder how much influence these religions and superstitions would have on these religious followers if the psychopathological symptoms associated with *shinkeishitsu* or hysteria were stripped from the symptoms of their disease.

Charcot (1877) once said that physicians should try anything that seems potentially effective. He was even ready to recommend a pilgrimage to the Holy Land. However, I believe he was gravely mistaken. If we limit ourselves to superficial observations and do not understand how a disorder is manifested and cured, or if we do not understand the pathology of anxiety disorders or hypochondriasis, our clients are likely to make a pilgrimage based on superstition—as do many clients. Therapists are encouraged to know how the psychopathology of *shinkeishitsu* is connected to the development of superstition.

The Role of Education in Promoting
Mental and Physical Health

My treatment for *shinkeishitsu* attempts to activate natural human abilities by promoting spontaneous mental and physical activities; treatment utilizes and redirects the pathological tendencies of individual clients, without denying the presence of these negative features. I believe that this method is useful for the education of children in general, and for those prone to *shinkeishitsu*. Montessori (1909) developed a method for educating children with intellectual impairments in Italy. The guiding principle of the Montessori method is one that encourages children's spontaneous activities, while allowing them to be free and self-reliant; conventional instilling or molding methods are discouraged.

My method of treatment does not expose clients to superficial, memory-oriented, or abstract knowledge; I think these methods are ineffective and even injurious to the day-to-day living of my clients. After treatment, clients frequently show great improvement in their academic records and comprehension of thoughtful books. More details on these phenomena and descriptions of clinical treatment of *shinkeishitsu* are found in my work, *Shinkeisuijaku-shō oyobi Kyōhakukannen no Konjihō (Radical Treatment of Neurasthenia and Obsessive Ideas)*.

The effects of my treatment on those with *shinkeishitsu* indicate that passive therapy methods alone are not effective for clients' mental and physical health, as these methods reinforce idle, weak, fragile, and less than resistant characters. Treatment requires active training methods and means to improve mental as well as physical health.

In this regard, please refer to my works *Shinkeishitsu oyobi Shinkeisuijaku-shō no Ryōhō (Treatment of Shinkeishitsu and Neurasthenia); Seishin Ryōhō Kogi (Lectures on Psychotherapy);* and *Shinkeisuijaku-shō oyobi Kyōhakukannen no Konjihō (Radical Treatment of Neurasthenia and Obsessive Ideas)*.

editor's glossary of
morita therapy terms

The glossary has been composed by the editor and is separate from the original text by MORITA Shoma.

Autosuggestion: This is an intellectual process wherein a person suggests to the self that s/he is ill; the person has a thought or sensation that is counter to her or his desire or comfort level and hence labels the experience as abnormal. Morita claimed that autosuggestion contributes to the development of "obsessive ideas" wherein the individual places fixed attention on her or his idea of illness and restricts awareness.

Ego or Ego-Centered: The term "ego" was translated into Japanese as *jiga* following Freud's reference. Apparently, the word *jiga* became popular in the 1920s among Japanese academics (particularly adherents of psychoanalysis) when referencing the "self." Essentially, when rendered from Chinese, *ji* is the self when it is not stained by the selfish or ego-centered *ga*. Although Freud's initial use of the term was more inclusive of self, Freud's later analytic use of the term interprets ego as a core functional subdivision of the mental apparatus. In contrast, Morita contends that by compartmental-izing mental structures, mental disorder is more likely to occur. In fact, mind=body; and from a Zen perspective, the conventional self is stained or enslaved by ego. Interestingly, Morita used the terms *jibun* and *jiko* in his book when referencing himself. (In Japanese, the subjective pronoun is given as *jibun* or *watashi*). Morita used the term ego as his point of contention. From a Morita perspective, the so-called ego is not to be strengthened; rather, the ego is to be transcended. Morita therapy is designed as a four-stage treatment in order to de-slave a person from ego since ego forms (and is the core of) the false self. The isolation-rest stage of treatment is instrumental in assisting the person toward experiencing true nature, true self, or body=mind. (As a historical note, just prior to her death in 1952, Karen Horney, M.D. was beginning to interpret ego in Morita's way).

Emotional Facts or Emotional Logic: Morita referred to the existence of "emotional facts" wherein one's true emotional state stands alone as its own fact, without the need for intellectual manipulation or interpretation. Reality-based judgments can be made by emotional logic when the existence of the core emotion is endorsed; following, intellectual knowledge can be applied to that fact. It is through the application of emotional logic that emotions are left to run their natural course and the "contradiction between ideas and reality" (*shisō-no-mujun*) is reconciled.

Extroversion: The concept of extroversion, as depicted by Morita, takes a broad meaning and extends beyond one's social relationships to include the animate and inanimate world. An "extroverted" individual would foster active relationships outside the self, not only with other people, but with the world of nature and the physical environment.

Feeling-Centered Attitude: This term is often misunderstood in Morita therapy. The emphasis is to be placed on the word *attitude*. Morita developed therapeutic methods to break down the client's feeling-centered attitudes, or the thoughts held about her or his feelings. Morita did not advocate the dismissal of feelings; rather, he encouraged his clients to fully experience the spontaneous nature and variety of their feelings. It is the thought or "attitude" one has about feelings that interferes with one's full and actual experience of feelings. Often times, a person labels a feeling or thinks that s/he should or should not feel a certain way;

these thoughts about feelings interfere with the authentic experience of feeling. It is these attitudes that are challenged by the therapy; the client learns (through the four-stage process of Morita therapy) to experience feelings naturally without interference by thoughts.

Hypochondriasis: Disorder in one's body=mind is precipitated by one's extreme fears of disease and potential death. Morita regards any fear of death and disability as a natural happening because fear indicates a human desire for life. Inklings of hypochondriasis, therefore, are evident in all people. The degree to which this fear is present determines the degree of abnormality. Hypochondriasis is divided into two types: (1) an "hypochondriacal tendency" that is an emotional base that originates during the course of one's life; and (2) a "hypochondriacal temperament" that is a congenital trait that predisposes one to hypochondriasis. It is the "hypochondriacal tendency" that is the primary feature of anxiety and obsessive disorders. Therapy is more effective with treating tendencies than temperaments.

Mind=Body: In order to decrease the tendency to dicotomize mind and body as two separate entities, the term is rendered as mind=body or body=mind. This shift in orientation has a profound impact on assessment and diagnosis. (For example, in Japan psychosomatic is often rendered as somapsychic).

Mushojū-shin: This is a Zen term used to describe healthy attention. If one wants to use the mind=body fully, one must extend the mind=body in all directions without attachment to a single focus. This does not imply a scattered mind, but rather complete alertness and aliveness. Morita attempts to remove the narrow focus of attention that one places on symptoms, as occurs in *shinkeishitsu,* and to increase spontaneous activity in the client's mind=body. Morita therapists are required personally to maintain this orientation of mind=body as their therapeutic reference in their practice.

Obsessive Disorder: This is a main feature of *shinkeishitsu* wherein cognitive conflict arises in a person when an initial sensation is accompanied by a fear of that sensation. There may be an awareness of meaninglessness, which increases fear and anxiety, much akin to an existential anxiety. Anticipatory fear furthers one's sensitivity to the sensation and increases one's anxiety. Any attempts to resist or deny the sensation only exacerbate the original fear or anxiety. Thus, one develops obsessive thinking.

Obsessive Thinking: This is different from obsessional thoughts. It is not the content of one's thinking that requires treatment; rather the filling of one's mind=body with thoughts requires quieting. The isolation bedrest stage of Morita therapy assists in quieting the client's obsessive thinking so that s/he can move into the successive stages of therapy.

Paroxysmal Neurosis: This is a subjective "attack" that often mimics a cardiac disorder; it is generated by the client's analytic thinking wherein fear and anxiety that increase the heart rate and subsequently increase the person's attention to the symptoms are interpreted as an attack. This neurosis becomes a cycle of objective and subjective focus and involves a cycle of obsessive ideas. Symptoms of paroxysmal neurosis are most similar to criteria set for Acute Stress Disorder in the Diagnostic and Statistical Manual IV (DSM-IV).

Shinkeishitsu: This is a prone-to-nervous personality with a hypochondriacal base, and is sometimes referred to as a "character disorder of the nervous type." It is often found in persons with an introverted temperament who are predisposed to a hypersensitive self-awareness of physical sensations. Those with *shinkeishitsu* have an understanding about the origin of their symptoms, in contrast to a person with hysteria who lacks such awareness. (*Shinkeishitsu* assumes that the person has the cognitive ability to experience this awareness.) *Shinkeishitsu* is classified into three pathological types: ordinary *shinkeishitsu*, paroxysmal neurosis, and obsessive ideas.

Shisō-no-Mujun **(Contradiction between Ideas and Reality):** This refers to the conflict that arises between one's intellect and reality as a person attempts to intellectually manipulate, modify, or deny what is real or actual according to her or his desires of how things "ought" to be. Therefore, contradiction occurs between experiential understanding or "emotional logic" (what is so, as emotional facts), and intellectual, ideational, or imaginary ideas (how one thinks things should or should not be). Contradiction by ideas creates *tendō-mōsō* or *akuchi* as described in Zen, which is "upside-down illusory thought" or "misplaced knowledge." It is the intention of Morita therapy to dismantle this contradiction by ideas and foster acceptance of facts as facts.

Shoichinen: This is a Zen term that indicates one's "original intention." This is sometimes referred to as *ichidan ronpo* or "one-step logic." Morita therapy attempts to decrease the client's critical judgment and analysis of her or his actual experience, as if one is a third-party observer of the self; the goal is to return the client to the state of experience before the moment of criticism.

Suffering: As consistent with Zen Buddhist rendering, Morita considered the cause of suffering to be the person's desire and attachment to illusion. One fact of the human condition is that all existence involves suffering. Morita's interpretation of suffering is consistent with the four illusions considered in Buddhism: the illusion that the phenomenal world is a source only for pleasure; the illusion that the phenomenal world is only good and pure, or bad and evil; the illusion that there exists a real ego; and the illusion that the phenomenal world is the only existing world.

Taitoku **(Experiential Embodied Understanding):** This is the knowledge obtained from one's direct experience and the experience of one's body in action. This is often compared to intellectual understanding or *rikai*. When a "contradiction between ideas and reality" is operating, the gap between experiential embodied understanding and intellectual understanding is great. It is this gap that increases the human struggle, and it is this gap that Morita therapy attempts to close.

Weak-Willed Disposition: This is a term developed by Morita to classify a particular characterological condition or personality disorder. The essential features of this condition include: a flat affect with lethargy and low motivation; an inability to feel delight; a lack of resolution for self-actualization or preservation; a tendency to become over enthusiastic or over idealizing; and a display of impulsive and reckless behaviors during over-idealized states. A weak-willed disposition is often found in those with *shinkeishitsu*. Symptoms of the weak-willed disposition seem most compatible with DSM-IV criteria that describes certain personality disorders. According to Morita, a personality disorder occurs when a person does not respond to the context of the moment.

supplementary section:*
theories about nature and
disorder that inform morita therapy

In order to understand the nature of anxiety disorders, a therapist requires knowledge of the interplay between the body and mind of a human being. For example, the therapist will want to distinguish between the physiology of a dull headache that commonly follows a person's long mid-day nap and the onset of a sharp headache in a client who obsesses about her or his symptoms.

There are various psychological theories that describe *shinkeishitsu*. For instance, anxiety symptoms can develop following traumatic experiences that induce fear, agony, or fury. Yet, many people experience psychic trauma and do not necessarily suffer from anxiety. Trauma-based theories do not explain this fact. Some theorists contend that neurosis results from a client's unconscious conflict (much like the formation of a complex) and emotional residue from past experiences. However, theories that highlight trauma and unconscious conflicts are based on causal relationships; these theories do not explain how or under what conditions an emotional experience becomes unconscious or subconscious. No one fully understands the relationship between emotional experience and the unconscious, or how the subconscious manifests itself in people who do not develop anxiety symptoms. When people have similar constitutions and experiences and live in the same environments, some

---

*This Supplementary Section is a collection of relevant sections from Part One and Morita's original 1928 text that has been mindfully compiled by the translator and editor.

of them suffer from anxiety-based disorders while others do not. All existing theories of neurosis fail to account for this important difference, including Freud's theory of neurosis and MATSUBARA's theory of the hypersensitive constitution and neurasthenia.

Hypochondriasis and Anxiety

To compensate for these shortcomings, I have developed a theory of neurosis that includes a hypochondriac base, or hypochondriac temperament. Former theorists have struggled to define neurosis. For instance, Beard (1880) advocated the term *neurasthenia,* which has been hotly debated among investigators. Jolly (1877) rejected the term *neurasthenia* and divided neurosis into hysteria and hypochondriasis. My theory also rejects the term *neurasthenia* and postulates that *anxiety-based disorders* emerge from one's over sensitivity to felt sensations or hypochondriasis. Hypochondriasis refers to a person's mental tendency or constitution; if hypochondriasis is severe, it may lead to a personality disorder.

Freud (1896b) contends that neurosis is caused by past psychic trauma. His treatment is designed to lead clients to understand the relationship between their neurosis and any relevant past history of psychic trauma. However, clients who suffer the same trauma do not necessarily develop neurosis. Freud believes that those who have introverted characters will suffer from neurosis, while those who have extroverted characters will escape neurosis. From my perspective, an extrovert stumbles while simultaneously running and looking up at an airplane in the sky, while an introvert walks carefully, watches her or his steps, but does not observe the plane. The extrovert pursues external goals with a purpose in mind, while the introvert is concerned with the self, her or his abilities, and the methods to attain certain goals. I think that different forms of neurosis occur naturally from one's temperament. For instance, hysteria is found in those with extroverted temperaments, and *shinkeishitsu* is found in those with introverted temperaments.

The introvert is very self-conscious and highly concerned with the details of her or his own physical and mental discomforts, abnormalities, and morbid sensations. This hypersensitivity tends to trigger hypochondriasis. Also, those with this kind of temperament are more likely to become dependent, depressed, or egocentric. In contrast, extroverts direct their attention to the social and physical environments and become very hasty in chasing their goals; they become careless, are continually overextended, and give no time to nurturing their health; they stand in marked contrast to those with *shinkeishitsu*. When either inclination predominates, the scales become one sided and the psychological imbalance becomes increasingly marked. A clear and active mind finds harmony between mental introversion and extroversion.

Hypochondriasis can develop from the care one receives and circumstances one encounters in childhood, and may occasionally develop by chance events or from traumatic life events (though siblings who grow up under the same circumstances and receive the same care often have different temperaments). However, a client's congenital tendency toward hypochondriasis tends to form the foundation from which *shinkeishitsu* emerges. In this regard, I view psychic trauma as a precursor to the development of *shinkeishitsu*.

What Is Hypochondriasis?

The diagnosis of hypochondriasis requires evidence of hypochondriacal thinking, such as worrying about one's fear of disease. The experience of "worrying" is a natural response to living and often reflects one's desire for continued existence. Therefore, some evidence of hypochondriasis is present in everyone. However, an initial natural psychological inclination can become abnormal and lead to *shinkeishitsu*. "Hypo" means under, beneath or down, and "chondor" means cartilage, which describes the epigastrium (the pit of the stomach) located under the extremity of the sternum cartilage. Usually during times of stress, a person will feel uneasy or apprehensive at this site. Hypochondriasis is a condition in which a person has many concerns about her or his body and fears having or contracting a disease.

Hypochondriasis is manifested according to the severity of one's fear of death and the means by which one's death might occur; these fears generate such phobias as the fear of disease, the fear of toxins or hazardous things, the fear of disasters or omens, the fear of unpleasant sensations, the fear of suffering, the fear of conflict, and the fear of fear or anticipatory anxiety. When a client fears death, s/he shows paroxysmal symptoms such as palpitation, anxiety, dizziness or fainting, and motor paralysis. Hypochondriasis is present in clients who have fears of developing a disease or disorder such as cancer, tuberculosis, syphilis, and psychosis.

When people fear the suffering that accompanies discomfort, they often manifest symptoms such as a headache, dizziness, disturbed consciousness, physical fatigue, tinnitus, distracted attention, nightmares, or insomnia. The location of these symptoms is related to visceral nervous functions involving blood circulation, hormone secretion, digestion, and reproduction. Parts of the nervous system that involve the sensory and motor organs, as well as mental activity, are commonly called neurasthenia. However, these symptoms are not organic or objective, but are subjective and result from *seishin-kōgo-sayō* (a vicious cycle of interaction between a person's attention to somatic symptoms, usually translated as "psychic interaction"). Symptoms that are increased by *seishin-kōgo-sayō* are not symptoms of neurasthenia as postulated by Beard (1880); I have called this disorder "pseudo-irritative hyposthenia" because it is not actually irritative hyposthenia, despite its appearance.

Obsessive Disorders

A person may suddenly become filled with fears of death, disease, or suffering when there is no presence of death or disease. S/he becomes introspective and critical of the self, and distorts physical sensations and ideas that most people take as normal phenomena. S/he believes the sensations are pathological, attempts to eliminate them, and falls into more conflict and suffering. This condition is exacerbated by a person's "obsessive ideas." Obsessive ideas occur when one is in a state of fear of suffering and agony. While in this state, a person develops anticipatory fear, and through autosuggestion invites more suffering voluntarily; this expands and worsens the original suffering within the mind=body. Thus, suffering is a progressive phenomenon, and an increase in obsessive ideas leads to an obsessive disorder. Because obsessive thinking involves a process of self-criticism, a person requires a certain degree of intellectual ability in order to self-reflect. Though rare, obsessive thinking may occur suddenly in some contexts. Usually, these symptoms do not occur in children or those with mental retardation because an intellectual capacity is not fully developed.

Neurasthenia, hypochondriasis, and obsessive disorders fall into the same category because all of them originate from a hypochondriacal base. These conditions fall under the general category of *shinkeishitsu* even though symptoms may vary. Clients with neurasthenia only suffer from the pain of symptoms, while those with hypochondriasis reject all suffering and develop anticipatory fear. Those with an obsessive disorder worry that they will not be able to eliminate their fears; in this regard, they focus all their attention on their own suffering.

Therapists need to understand the pathology of anxiety disorders before they apply treatment to eliminate the hypochondriac base that accompanies the disorder. In addition, it is necessary to determine therapy according to clients' presenting symptoms. Therapy for those with neurasthenia is less complicated than therapy for those with an obsessive disorder.

The Subjective Nature of Anxiety

Symptoms reported by those with anxiety disorders are essentially subjective in nature, unless mental and physical fatigue or other complications are present. Clients, therefore, commonly describe their symptoms with subjective terms, such as having a sense of headache, a sense of dizziness, a feeling of being easily distracted, or a feeling of being tired because of insomnia or nightmares. For example, when the therapist asks for details about the client's dizziness or headache, the client may complain by saying: "I know I don't look like I'm ill, but I'm really suffering from unbearable pains." This provides evidence that the symptoms are not concrete and medically objective. A client occasionally says, "No one else suffers as much as I do." I tell such clients that, "Those who suffer as greatly as you do are the most unhappy, miserable people in the world. If ordinary people have such sufferings, they can hardly stand up and talk. In your case, in spite of your tremendous suffering, you make ordinary conversation with others and engage in your work. This shows that you are very courageous. In other words, a miserable person can be, at the same time, functional and courageous. There is only a hairline distance to leap to enable you to replace your complaining mind with a mind filled with confidence and joy."

If the condition of *shinkeishitsu* is compared before and after application of my method of treatment, it becomes clear that the symptoms are subjective. As a result of clinical examination, it is also clear that there are no significant differences in attention and memory, or mental and physical fatigue between these clients and healthy individuals. In fact, research by Ziehen (1908), Weygandt (1905), and DuBois (1908) show little agreement on the results of examination that include muscle fatigue curves of ergography, experiments on ocular fatigue, and other mental efficiency tests; this is possibly because they did not diagnose and differentiate between fatigue caused by neurasthenia and that caused by *shinkeishitsu*.

Seishin-kōgo-sayō

During the development of *shinkeishitsu, seishin-kōgo-sayō* takes place via the following mental process: when a person's attention is fixated on a sensation, awareness of that sensation becomes sharper and sensitivity to the sensation increases. The mutual interaction between sensation and attention heightens the person's awareness of the self and the sensation.

Shinkeishitsu manifests itself in various symptoms, such as experiencing a headache; feeling dizzy upon standing; feeling fuzzy in one's consciousness or distracted in attention; experiencing palpitations, distension of the stomach, or fear of contracting a disease; feeling shame in public; feeling lust toward someone of the opposite sex; and experiencing an anxiety attack, paralysis, insomnia, or neuralgialike symptoms. When symptoms are traced back to their beginning, they are found to be common sensations and emotions that healthy individuals routinely experience. Normal experiences include: feeling a dull headache following excessive work or sleep; feeling an unpleasantness in the stomach after eating more than one's body needs; feeling a flush in the face when standing close to a person with whom one feels infatuated; feeling shakes or chills when witnessing the sudden death of a person; feeling a cramp in one's side when running, and so on.

Clients with *shinkeishitsu* tend to regard any of these normal conditions as a morbid abnormality because of their hypochondriac tendencies. As their fear increases, they develop anticipatory anxiety. This cycle further aggravates their sensitivity via the process of *seishin-kōgo-sayō* and results in their chronic fixation on symptoms. Dull headaches, insomnia, and dizziness can occur from excessive studying as well as cranial trauma and influenza. Hypersensitive reactions in those with *shinkeishitsu* are not of an actual physical nature but result from one's excessive preoccupation with such discomfort due to one's hypochondriac tendency. Therefore, this is regarded as "pseudo-sensitivity."

As described above, it is most appropriate to diagnose, explain, and treat symptoms of *shinkeishitsu* by attending to the accompanying hypochondriac base and the mental process of *seishin-kōgo-sayō*. Symptoms of *shinkeishitsu* may coincide with actual symptoms that accompany diseases or traumatic events; however, symptoms of *shinkeishitsu* persist well after the physical condition or trauma has been healed. Once symptoms have been set via *seishin-kōgo-sayō*, clients remain trapped in their subjective perception and believe in the actual existence of their symptoms. They believe in the existence of their symptoms as strongly as they believe in the existence of their dreams. Confined in their subjectivity, they suffer continually from the agony of their symptoms. There is an old saying, "The object that I feel to be a ghost is actually a withered pampas grass."

A client may be able to reduce her or his preoccupation with symptoms that are subjective in nature with the help of a lay therapist. However, if a professional clinical assessment and diagnosis is not made at the onset of treatment, random implementation of psychotherapy may be hazardous to the client.

The Emotion of Fear

The emotion of fear occurs when a person anticipates that s/he will suffer misfortune or be exposed to danger. When a person is startled, autonomic responses occur wherein breathing becomes shallow, the diaphragm raises, the tongue cramps, abdominal strength decreases, the body shivers, or the person feels anxiety and finds her or his attention easily distracted. If the person does not focus atten-

tion exclusively on her or his symptoms, then s/he will believe the symptoms are naturally related to the momentary
experience of shock. However, if the client places attention
on the self and remains overly aware of palpitations or dizziness associated with the previous emotion, symptoms will
be perpetuated. If the person fears heart disease, palpitations
will develop and increase. If the person fears apoplexy, then
s/he will generate symptoms of being easily distracted, of
entering a twilight state, of feeling dizzy or faint. These conditions are occasionally associated with symptoms such as
paralysis of the leg, quivering (sometimes described as a
spasm), chills, cold sweats, xerostomia, aphasia, intrathoracic pain, and acute anxiety attacks. All these reactions occur in response to "the shock of fear," but the manner in
which a client complains relates to the direction in which
s/he focuses attention.

Panic attacks have been associated with hysteria, the
"hysterical ball" (the feeling of having a ball stuck in the
throat), chest pain, latero-abdominal pain, and gastric or
uterine spasms or *shaku*. Though the client feels pain at a
particular site, the pain is not an actual spasm of the stomach or uterus. There are extreme cases of women who are
mistakenly diagnosed as being in child-bearing labor because their fears and reported pains are so intense.

Various conditions may be prompted by the emotion
of fear. For instance, pain can be felt as cramping in the
latero-abdominal region, or heart attack sensations may develop via *seishin-kōgo-sayō*. Oftentimes, clients do not recognize the first attack of symptoms as a phenomenon that is
naturally related to their fear. Also, they do not understand
the relationship between the attack and their past experiences of fear because their minds are dominated by an intense fear of disease. Their attention is focused exclusively
on their fear, which makes it impossible for them to make
calm observations about themselves in relation to their fear
and pain. When clients suffer from the first panic attack,
they are trapped by their own fear of subsequent attacks.

Thus, they develop similar attacks whenever a similar context in their environment arises. The past experience of pain becomes reenacted in the present reality. In dreams, a person can experience ideas, emotions, or pains as if they were real. Similarly, clients' reactions to their fear are comparable to the phenomenon of believing that dreams or hallucinations are real.

If these symptoms are interpreted as resulting from an unconscious or subconscious processes (as many theorists believe), then other symptoms of anxiety disorders including headache, dizziness, and obsessive thinking could also be explained by theories of consciousness. However, clients do not make therapeutic progress simply by recognizing the origins of their hypochondriac base, or by understanding the process of *seishin-kōgo-sayō*, or by making the so-called unconscious conscious.

Persistence of Unpleasant Emotions

Symptoms like heart palpitation are easily understood as resulting from *seishin-kōgo-sayō* when the development and course of attacks are identified and studied in great detail. Other conditions like simple headache, dizziness, and complicated obsessive disorders can be explained similarly. For example, one may notice a dull feeling in her or his head following excessive work or sleep or prolonged child delivery, or one may be sensitized to an abnormal sensation after the onset of enteritis.

Attention and sensation mutually stimulate and aggravate each other. Long after the actual cause of the symptom has disappeared, the person feels discomfort because s/he focuses the mind on anticipating pain in the future (anticipatory fear); thus, s/he generates repeated headaches through such a tense state of mind. Common wisdom demonstrates that a person's condition may become worse if s/he stays indoors for long periods of time; thus, some recuperation strategies aggravate conditions. As clients attempt to treat their own symptoms, they may self-prescribe lots of sleep and restricted exercise or work; this type of exclusive rest treatment will cause the human body to become weak and the spirit to decline. The person will eventually feel more fatigued, mentally dull, or confused. As an old saying goes, "Even steel gathers rust, if it is not used."

People feel dizzy for various reasons, such as when standing up suddenly after reading in a sitting position for a long time, when getting out of bed following a fever, when looking down from a bridge at a rapidly moving stream, or when watching a car drive past them at a high speed. If a person associates such events with a fear of disease and ruminates about this in her or his mind, then s/he will suffer in daily life. The best example of this phenomenon is seasickness. In people who are prone to seasickness, their physical shaking motion caused by the rolling and pitching of the ship does not disappear immediately upon disembarkation. The symptoms of anxiety disorders persist in a similar way.

An obsessive disorder can develop when a person regards a perfectly natural phenomenon as abnormal or morbid and develops associated fears; this process eventually aggravates the symptoms through *seishin-kōgo-sayō*. For instance, a person may accidentally blush with shame during a public ceremony, fear contamination while caring for a sick person who suffers from dysentery, or become afraid that s/he might accidentally harm someone with a gun while cleaning it. Any of these incidents may become the focus of a person's excessive attention. Consequently, the person develops anticipatory fear associated with the incident and attends to every minute detail in her or his thoughts and behavior. Attention and anxiety alternately reinforce each other. Eventually, the person develops an anxiety disorder or phobia around the fear of blushing, germs, or weapons.

Once a client is preoccupied with one specific incident and develops obsessive thoughts and repetitive behaviors, her or his attention is focused exclusively on the self. Thus, the client's sphere of attention is extremely narrow. This is exemplified by the saying, "A hunter in pursuit of a deer sees no hills." NOMURA Waihan, who died with his lover in a "love suicide" or *shinjū*, stated prior to his own suicide, "No one can know the mind of one who yearns only for a world of eternity." Such people live entirely in a subjective centered world and have no room for anything else. They may feel pain when pricked with a pin but feel nothing when they witness another person being pierced by a spear. They cannot empathize when others are in the same circumstances as themselves; they do not comprehend the fact that other people have levels of anxiety and pain similar to their own. In general, clients with anxiety disorders often think that they are alone in their unique suffering. This is one distinguishing feature of anxiety-based disorders and hypochondriasis.

It is impossible for a client with anxiety to detach her or himself from suffering, to realistically compare the self with others, and to sympathize with others. Just as a starving person rarely feeds others, those with anxiety-based disorders have no room to care for others because they feel overwhelmed by their own suffering and fear. Hence, these clients become egocentric, irritable, impatient, and depressed whenever they compare themselves to others, and they are unable to harmonize with other people. Depression and irritation are secondary characteristics of anxiety disorders and arise from a person's errors in critical thinking. For example, a client diagnosed with a depressive disorder will generally develop pessimistic attitudes as a secondary response to her or his depression. In contrast, a client with an anxiety disorder will manifest depression as a secondary characteristic based on her or his primary pessimistic orientation to life.

A person with an anxiety-based disorder has no characterological or biological cause for irritability, unlike those who exhibit weak-willed characters or intellectual disabilities. In contrast to those who have impulsive control disorders, those with anxiety disorders rarely resort to violence. Violent behaviors emitted by those with anxiety disorders occur after much consideration and it is rarely the result of faulty impulse control; their behaviors may result from rigid logic and are not impulsive; a violent act serves as a means to an end. If violence is otherwise, it is due to the presence of another disorder and the person does not have an anxiety-based disorder with hypochondriasis (or pure *shinkeishitsu*).

Those with anxiety-based disorders who seek solitude and avoid contact with people are often afraid that their distress will be aggravated by others. This is a secondary condition and may be evidence of a personality disorder. Also, the fear of contracting an imagined disease is a secondary condition. When there is evidence of a weak will, it is a false or pseudo-weakness rather than an actual reduction in the person's will power. Thus, the assessment of an anxiety-based disorder requires critical attention by the therapist to these differences.

Consciousness, Attention, and Association

I do not use the word *conscious* to define human ability or action. Also, I do not use such phrases as "an act of consciousness," or "a function of the subconscious." I think that consciousness is the state of mind at the time. I am not satisfied with the Freudian and teleological explanations of psychological phenomena, and I am not satisfied by theorists who put "consciousness" into a fixed grid of categories. Rather, I try to observe and describe a phenomenon as it exists naturally, scientifically, and realistically.

Through a function of association, a person's responses to internal and external stimuli are embossed into her or his body as the so-called conscious and unconscious experiences. From this "storehouse of collected experiences," certain optimal conditions trigger physical and mental activity.*

---

*It is interesting to note that Morita was writing about a collective kind of consciousness experience decades before Carl Jung discussed the "collective unconscious." Morita's concept, in particular, maintains a mind=body perspective and embraces consciousness as an undifferentiated phenomenon.

For example, a person will withdraw a hand from a fire; s/he will jump when startled by an unexpected sound; s/he may reflect on suicide at Kegon Falls (a familiar site in Japan for suicides); s/he may think dark thoughts when depressed; s/he may contemplate God when seeing the ideogram that means "love"; or s/he may believe s/he has dysentery when sick with diarrhea. Thus, in response to associations that are triggered by internal and external stimuli, one's intellect, emotion, and volition are constantly changing. Furthermore, a person's ideas, moods, and activities promptly become stimuli that induce more activity and change; thus, the mind is naturally in constant motion. Changes occur in the human mind=body, night and day, regardless of whether a so-called consciousness or unconsciousness is recognized.

When internal or external stimuli beyond a certain degree impinge on the human body, changes occur in the body that lead to reflexes or movements in the autonomic nervous system. For example, when the bladder becomes full during sleep, a person moves her or his legs to shift a sleeping position. When one feels a hair on her or his face, s/he brushes it away. When the degree of stimulation is increased above a certain level, an awareness occurs within the self. The dividing line between the occurrence and non-occurrence of self-awareness may be called the "stimulation threshold" from the viewpoint of stimulation, the "sensation threshold" from the viewpoint of self-awareness, or the "consciousness threshold" from the realm of consciousness. The level of the threshold between stimulation and awareness varies according to conditions and circumstances. In some cases, a very slight stimulation comes into one's awareness, while on other occasions a strong stimulation does not prompt awareness. The relationship depends first on the individual's mental and physical condition and secondly on the environment and degree of stimulation.

Mental and physical states, such as alertness, fatigue, weight loss and gain, cheerfulness, and tenseness are continually changing and vary from one person to another. Therefore, if two people are walking on the same street, one may notice a bookstore, while the other may be aware of a liquor store or bakery; another person may become so absorbed in her or his imagination that s/he notices little. Consider the following saying in relation to this: "The mind of the common person is awakened by gain, while that of a sage awakens to justice." Mental tension and the focus of attention elicits many different responses. For instance, a mother who is sleeping beside a sick infant will awaken if the infant coughs, but she may not be awakened by the roar of thunder. She is not awakened by the thunder because it is outside the locus of her attention. Additionally, a primary school child who is looking forward to a school picnic has no trouble waking up early on the day of the picnic, whereas most school days s/he wants to sleep late.

I think that the process of fixing one's attention brings an awareness of the passing of time as if one is in the state of being half-asleep and half-awake; in this state, the child wakes up at the required time. Consider the saying, "The *samurai* is awakened even by the sound of a horse bit." The *samurai* (military officer or warrior), the mother who sleeps with her sick baby, and the school child do not sleep in a natural relaxed way. They keep themselves in tension by remaining in a ready-to-spring physical position so that they can easily react to a very slight stimulus.

Thus, a person senses matters above the awareness threshold at each moment during the constant flux in mental activity. The mind flows constantly in and out of awareness and is compared to a revolving lantern or the wavering reflections of sunbeams on the rotating water of a watermill. If one explains symptoms merely by the terms *unconscious* or *subconscious* and overlooks the continual unfolding process of mental activity, there is little possibility for practical treatment. In essence, knowledge of the location of an underground mine is useless without tapping its lode.

Object-Centered Consciousness

Mental activity moves spontaneously and instinctively toward adaptation and self-preservation. Consciousness is like water that flows down through a valley, breaks on the rocks, makes a deep pool, fills a river, and eventually enters the sea. The awareness threshold changes according to one's level of applied exertion and amount of effort and tension required to meet demands. The mind attends naturally to new stimuli or experiences and gives less awareness to habitual activities. To play music or make handicrafts, for example, requires great care at first; however, once one becomes skilled, one is less aware of the details of the activity. When a Japanese person picks up beans with chopsticks, s/he is quite unaware of how s/he is using her or his fingers. Thus, attention and awareness are oriented centrifugally toward the object alone. In other words, "A hunter in pursuit of a deer sees no hills." The text of a sutra similarly says that "One who collects honey will know no deep pits at foot, while paying attention only to honey."

When we catch a ball, we concentrate on the ball more than our hands. When we are about to hit something, our mind is focused in that direction alone, and we are not aware of the movement of our hands. When a person is focused on the feeling of surprise or fear, the mind is not conscious of any cause and effect process. I hypothesize that this feature of consciousness is the "peripheral feature" or "object-centeredness" of attention or consciousness. As a result of this object-centeredness, a person frequently misunderstands the relationship between a result or a fact, and the condition or process that causes an opposite response. For instance, most people think that the biceps muscle of the arm swells up to assist the bending of the arm. However, in fact, the muscle contracts with a resulting inflexion of the forearm. Such misunderstandings occur frequently by theorists who describe routine mental activity.

Conscious attention can be observed from temporal and spatial perspectives. With regard to time, the awareness threshold varies constantly in response to mental and physical activity. With regard to space, attention can be compared to the visual field. When one's attention is fixed on a certain point, her or his consciousness is the clearest at that point. Awareness gradually becomes less focused in the margins of one's field of view, and eventually the periphery disappears altogether. One can fixate attention on a single point with a tense mind, or one can release her or his mental tension and focus on the point in a relaxed manner. The point of focus will become clear or cloudy and appear or disappear according to changes in one's consciousness. Changes in consciousness are due to the rhythmic nature of human attention. A person may not be conscious of feeling fear in spite of acting afraid, or one may not feel courage in spite of being inspired to act with strength. One may not be aware of criticism or judgment by others because s/he adheres to particular beliefs.

Function of Suggestion

The process of inducing a hypnotic trance is related to attention. Initially, attention is directed when a person's mind focuses on an object by such methods as the steady-gaze technique. Also, consciousness and attention expand as the client focuses on the hypnotist's guidance by means of verbal suggestion. Herein, the client can enter into the so-called state of no-mind and begin to act according to the hypnotist's guidance without making critical evaluations.

An individual's philosophy or belief system is developed and influenced by words and behaviors of others, by the external environment, and by internal sensations or ideas. When one develops a belief system, one makes evaluations or judgments intuitively and emotionally. One's beliefs influence one's mind=body. When emotional judgment is employed, attention is focused on only one point. This results in a narrowed consciousness, just like the concentric shrinkage of the visual field. However, a belief system can serve to free the person from outside influences that impinge on her or his mind, body, and behaviors and break down critical judgments via suggestion. (Any suggestion that one gives to oneself that originates from within the self is called "autosuggestion.")

When clients fix their attention on a single idea (or hold fixed ideas based on autosuggestion), they lose the freedom of activity to attend to their surroundings and enter into a state of extended consciousness or active attention. As a result, they are trapped by their own ideas, which interpret reality. If a client with *shinkeishitsu* fears having a dull headache or thinks something will happen to bring shame, then her or his expectation is apt to become reality. The client does not see the actual circumstances because her or his attention is focused on the feared outcome. The dreaded outcome is facilitated by the person via her or his autosuggestion. Various types of attacks described by those with *shinkeishitsu* occur via autosuggestion and anticipatory fear. In a client who has a previous history of heart attack, her or his anticipatory fear suddenly reappears and becomes a felt reality when attention is fixated on fear. Also, dreams seem real because no attention is focused on the external environment during sleep, and one's consciousness is extremely narrowed. A client with *shinkeishitsu* may view her or his abnormality like a dream after healing. This phenomenon happens because the condition was a subjective fiction.

Fixation of Attention

Clients with *shinkeishitsu* sometimes complain of frequent dreams and obsessive thoughts. These complaints can be explained by a state of mind caused by one's fixed attention. Detailed self-observation shows us that we generally dream just before waking. However, people are not normally aware of this fact and do not remember their dreams. Therefore, when people say they have not dreamed, it merely indicates that their dreams are not remembered. Because the constant stimuli of daily life impinge on us soon after waking, consciousness is continually changing and one naturally forgets the contents of dreams. Though dreams are not readily retained in awareness, one can be trained to remember dreams by practicing self-observation. Clients with *shinkeishitsu* think that they have many dreams because they concentrate on dreams as evidence of poor sleep when they fear insomnia. Therefore, after successful therapy, they respond naturally; in this way, they do not remember all their dreams, do not worry about the content of their dreams, and no longer fear insomnia.

The same sort of explanation applies to obsessive disorders. While shame and blushing occur naturally, most people do not linger in these experiences or are not self aware of these responses in daily life because their field of consciousness changes in response to new stimuli. While predictions, fortune telling, and superstitions may or may not come true, putting belief in these notions will increase their probability because attention is so narrowly focused. If people give no particular credence to them, predicted events are less likely to come true because more comprehensive comparison and consideration can be made. Symptoms of *shinkeishitsu* are like a "philosophy." They develop via autosuggestion when a person maintains fixed attention on a particular incident. Anxiety-laden symptoms are often subjective experiences, though the client believes her or his symptoms are pathological.

Classification of Anxiety-Based Disorders *(Shinkeishitsu)*

According to my view on the nature of *shinkeishitsu,* I have developed a classification system of three pathological types, from simple to complex: (1) ordinary *shinkeishitsu*; (2) paroxysmal neurosis; and (3) obsessive ideation or obsessive disorder.

Originally, I included hypochondriasis as a fourth category of *shinkeishitsu* but later excluded it because I found it to be a differentiating feature of ordinary *shinkeishitsu*. I have tentatively divided *shinkeishitsu* into "somatically hypersensitive disposition" and "mentally hypersensitive disposition," a distinction that has been made for convenience. A mentally hypersensitive disposition is a prerequisite for *shinkeishitsu*; without it, the formation of *shinkeishitsu* symptoms is impossible. The somatically hypersensitive state can occur in individuals who have intellectual disabilities, or when someone is in delicate health. It may be especially marked in some cases just before or after the onset of schizophrenia.

I regret that most investigators still do not understand that the nature of obsessive disorders is similar to that of ordinary *shinkeishitsu*. This is well demonstrated by the results of my treatment, which show that both types of *shinkeishitsu* are cured in the same number of days by the same method. Though an obsessive disorder is regarded as difficult to treat by routine methods of therapy, it is less likely to recur following my method of treatment. The symptoms of *shinkeishitsu* transfer or amalgamate across disorders. Cases of ordinary *shinkeishitsu* show symptoms of obsessive disorders, and cases of obsessive disorders show symptoms of ordinary *shinkeishitsu*. Therefore, differential diagnosis requires attention to the core disorder.

Rejection of So-Called Neurasthenia

The terms *acquired neurasthenia* or *exogenous neurasthenia* are unreasonable in my opinion, and are likely to give rise to misunderstanding. These terms merely describe a person's state of chronic or acute fatigue, or mental and physical collapse. During fatigued conditions, the normal equilibrium of metabolism is disturbed due to mental or physical overwork, trauma following an accident, emotional agitation, or under nourishment. Initially, the client almost always suffers weight loss, which is the first marker for identifying neurasthenia; the client's mental and physical functions become progressively weaker as described by Beard (1880). I think that the condition of neurasthenia is observed in various states as a general symptom of fatigue or physical ailment. Thus, it is not prudent to differentiate this condition specifically as neurasthenia.

People occasionally think that mental and physical overwork are two entirely different things, but this is like regarding fatigue of the arms as different from fatigue of the legs. Therefore, I do not see any reason to label mental fatigue as neurasthenia. The symptoms of neurasthenia disappear as the client recovers from mental and physical fatigue or illness. For instance, the pain in the legs and lower back that result from climbing Mt. Fuji recover in several days. The headache and insomnia that result from preparing for an examination recover similarly. However, if a person is dominated by an hypochondriac mood and fixes attention on the morbid sensation, the symptoms become increasingly complicated in accordance with her or his predisposition to *shinkeishitsu*. Evidence of *shinkeishitsu* is present when the person recovers from fatigue and is restored to physical health because the subjective symptoms persist. These symptoms of *shinkeishitsu* are caused by mental fixation. When this mental fixation is assessed, a prognosis and method of treatment becomes clear.

Ordinary Shinkeishitsu

"Ordinary" *shinkeishitsu* is the basic type and may be regarded as *shinkeishitsu* in a narrow sense. It has conventionally been regarded as a congenital disorder, a personality or character disorder, or cerebral neurasthenia. Because neurasthenia has been classified into various types (including cerebral, spinal, cardiac, gastrointestinal, and reproductive), *shinkeishitsu* is sometimes misdiagnosed as a specific type of neurasthenia. I think that the system of classifying neurasthenia is impractical because a symptom-based assessment offers little clinical understanding of the characteristics and treatment of the disorder. Also, the therapist fixes her or his attention solely on the client's presenting symptoms rather than assessing the client's tendency or process.

Consider the case of a client who suffered from constipation and gastric atony. He had bowel movements only with the use of laxatives from the age of fourteen to the age of twenty-four. In spite of five months of treatment at a gastrointestinal clinic, the client did not recover. After being admitted to my clinic, all drugs were withdrawn. For the first nine days of his forty-day treatment, constipation persisted, but thereafter bowel movements occurred; eventually, spontaneous bowel movements took place approximately every other day. Similarly, I treated a forty-five-year-old man who had suffered from tenesmus alvi and had mucous stools for four or five years. Though he had a bowel movement every morning, it took him at least one hour to complete. He was admitted to a gastrointestinal clinic and was treated for more than two months under the diagnosis of rectal catarrh, but no recovery was achieved. After a single examination, I told him to stay in the bathroom for no more than five minutes. The client complied with my suggestion and recovered completely within one week. All such conditioned symptoms, which begin with mental fixation on a certain abnormal sensation are aggravated by an abnormal pattern of daily life and erroneous treatment of the symptoms.

Physicians in various fields are apt to consider the symptoms of *shinkeishitsu* as direct causal relationships according to their own specialty, be it ophthalmology, gastroenterology, urology, or venereology. If a physician assesses the client's mental fixation on the symptom rather than the symptom alone, s/he can prescribe methods that improve the client's mental attitude and lifestyle.

Paroxysmal Neurosis

I define "paroxysmal neurosis" as a condition that is characterized by various painlike attacks, including palpitation, weakness in the extremities, dizziness, a rush of blood to the head, fainting spells, acute anxiety, chills, trembling, gastrospasm, and hysterospasm. All these attacks are subjective in nature. For example, the symptom of weakness in the extremities does not show evidence of motor paralysis, and the symptom of fainting does not involve clouding of consciousness. Some clients occasionally complain of attacks of spasms, but their attacks are similar to the neurological shuddering response associated with fear.

The cause of these attacks is the agitation by fear. The painlike attacks are not based on actual pain and may be regarded as an illusion or a dream of pain in the awakened state. Such attacks are called *shaku* (convulsions) in Japanese. Paroxysmal neurosis may resemble hysteria and requires differential diagnosis of the client's tendency toward hysteria and *shinkeishitsu*. Also, when compared to hysteria, treatment and recovery is easier for those with *shinkeishitsu*.

Distinguishing an Obsessive Disorder from Compulsive Acts

I have defined "obsessive ideas" as a mental conflict wherein a client believes a particular sensation or emotion is evidence of a morbid abnormality, and s/he resists feeling or thinking about such a sensation or impression. An obsessive disorder, therefore, cannot exist in the absence of mental conflict. Clients will recover from an obsessive disorder only if they experience pain as it actually exists, while eliminating efforts of resistance directed against their pain. The onset of delusion in the early stage of schizophrenia may look similar to the belief system that operates in those with obsessive disorders; however, this similarity is rare and is apt to be erroneously diagnosed. In schizophrenia, there is no clear mental conflict that can be assessed.

Investigators generally associate obsessive disorders with the presence of a phobia or compulsive act. In my opinion, it is difficult to treat compulsive behaviors because they are almost always refractory. Unlike obsessive disorders, compulsive disorders are hardly associated with the pain of mental conflict and most acts are impulsive.

A client with a compulsive disorder acts directly from a fixed emotion derived from things like omens or excessive cleanliness; s/he merely acts to diminish the anxiety associated with these conditions. Such a client lacks deep self-awareness or recognition of the illness and is rarely amenable to recovery through treatment. It is sometimes difficult to differentiate obsessive disorders from compulsive disorders if several years have passed since the onset or if these disorders occur well into adulthood. However, it is possible to differentiate the two conditions on the basis of a client's mental conflict, impulse control, and initiative to enter treatment voluntarily.

There are many kinds of phobias that have their foundation in *shinkeishitsu*. Agoraphobia has been known for a long time in Japan. This refers to anxiety caused by being in particular spaces and places. A client with this condition may fear specific places, such as open spaces or crowded places, and is obsessed with the possibility of experiencing dizziness, fainting, motor paralysis, cardioplegia, and confusion when in these situations. Such clients generally fear going out and may be unable to go to a public bath. Many of these cases represent paroxysmal neurosis rather than an obsessive disorder, which does not adequately describe the nature of the client's condition.

The fear of blushing has been known since Casper described erythrophobia in 1846. In 1902, Hartenberg classified anxiety about blushing into three types: (1) general blushing, or a blushing upon meeting others that is not associated with fear; (2) fear of blushing; (3) and a constant fear of blushing. However, this classification is impractical because it focuses exclusively on blushing. Anxiety about blushing indicates a fear of being concerned with others' judgment or attention, and is an obsessive idea that is more akin to a fear of shyness. One type of concern related to blushing centers on being watched by others. It is associated with countless and various patterns: serious confusion about how to appear and act in public; a fear of underarm sweating; a fear of stuttering; a feeling of shame about not being able to look someone in the face, or as I term, a fear of direct gaze; a fear of having to answer to questions from others due to over-concern with how one responds; unpleasant feelings like having an insect crawling in the mouth; anxiety due to a fear of passing wind in public; a fear of shaking due to shyness; or ochlophobia. Given these varied patterns, I discourage therapists from concentrating solely on facial flushing when considering their clients' obsessive ideas. I once treated a student who was worried about seeing the tip of his own nose. This case serves as a good example of the psychology of obsessive disorders because the client considered something entirely ordinary to be a morbid abnormality.

Based on my clinical practice, I have identified other obsessive foci: fears of omens, impurities, toxins, germs, and illnesses; syphilophobia; fear of leprosy; fear of psychosis; fear of theft wherein the person fears being robbed or fears becoming a thief; fear of murder wherein the person fears killing or being killed; fear of desecrating a deity; fear of grudges wherein the person fears incurring a grudge or being unable to forget a grudge against another; pyrophobia; claustrophobia; acrophobia; fear of pointed objects; fear of particular numbers; fear of a memory lapse; fear of immorality; fear of making mistakes; fear of misunderstanding or doubting; fear of calculation and reading; fear of the night; fear of sex or urination; and fear of being thrown off from the earth by its rotation. There are far too many fears to list.

Circumstantial Influences on Anxiety Disorders

HEISABURO Takashima has written about "first impressions." When a teacher scolds a primary school child, the event may have a lasting negative effect on the child. This is similar to the complex (Komplex) described by Freud in 1915.

MARUI, who based his studies on Freud's theory of psychoanalysis, advocated that the care received in childhood is closely associated with the development of neurosis. SHIMODA also discussed the importance of child-rearing influences on the development of *shinkeishitsu*, explaining that *shinkeishitsu* results from poor care in childhood. This fact is widely recognized. The difference between nurturing and harmful care in childhood is similar to the difference between trees that are allowed to grow naturally and bonsai trees that are artificially dwarfed. However, the correlation is not perfect, and no direct cause-effect relationship seems to exist. For example, brothers who grow up in the same environment have natural differences and develop different temperaments.

With regard to the so-called first impression and Freud's idea of complex, individuals have a different reaction to the same event based on their individual differences in temperament. Thus, the individual's inherent temperament needs to be taken into consideration in determining the influences on the development of *shinkeishitsu*. In addition, the lingering of emotional states varies according to the unique personality of each individual, such as fear of earthquakes and disasters, or sorrow over a broken heart. Thus, the same event brings different emotional responses depending on whether one is intellectually impaired, weak willed, normal or anxiety-laden.

Some clients show a marked anxiety-prone temperament from the time they are infants, regardless of how well cared for they may be. In contrast, some may not show any manifestations of this temperament, but for some reason develop *shinkeishitsu*. In certain extreme cases, the person may suffer from marked *shinkeishitsu* for the first time at the age of forty or fifty; although these cases frequently manifest as acute anxiety disorders.

Someone who has not shown a particularly anxiety-prone temperament may experience a certain psychic trauma, then suddenly become strongly overwhelmed by a hypochondriac mood; s/he may succumb to this mood and be unable to get free. These cases reflect the desire for life and the fear of death that are natural to all human beings. Someone born with an even and calm disposition, for example, who has never thought of life, death, or religious matters, may suddenly believe in ghosts and psychic phenomena and become extremely superstitious. There are some who become superstitious as a result of their congenital temperament and others who become superstitious by a chance occurrence in the course of their life. In such cases, my theory of the hypochondriac base refers to an emotional underpinning that can originate in the course of a person's life.

Generally speaking, *shinkeishitsu* occurs in those with a character sensitivity that predisposes a person to self-attentiveness and hypochondriasis. If sufficient mental development has not yet been established for self-observation or critical evaluation, the complex symptoms of *shinkeishitsu* or obsessive disorders are unlikely to occur. However, such symptoms and ideas occasionally increase with advancing age, particularly following adolescence. Habitual headaches may occur or obsessive ideas may develop for no particular reason, or symptoms of *shinkeishitsu* may manifest because of an illness, disaster, or strong emotion. If a hypersensitive constitution is present in such cases, the symptoms will be increasingly complicated. If mental and physical fatigue is added, the symptoms are even more severe. In the treatment of *shinkeishitsu*, the therapist needs to diagnose the symptoms, attend to the client's need for physical and mental rest, and perform a special treatment for the underlying condition of *shinkeishitsu*. My four-stage treatment can increase clients' mental and physical resistance to illness, particularly when they have hypersensitive dispositions. Calcium therapy, organotherapy, and nutrition therapy are insufficient as fundamental therapies in the treatment of *shinkeishitsu*.

Reconceptualizing Personality Disorders

A deficient personality refers to a person's limited ability to adapt to changes in human and environmental relationships and life circumstances and an inability to think without distortion. Those with deficient characters cannot be regarded as either ill or healthy because they display an intermediate condition between health and illness.

Healthy individuals have a wide range of abilities for meeting the demands of daily living; they adapt themselves readily to change, develop themselves, and respond to other people. Health is not based on a single characteristic, such as having a sound body, good memory, or vivid imagination.

Those with so-called personality disorders adapt themselves poorly to circumstances and respond to the external world with extreme sensitivity or dullness. Therefore, they frequently suffer from physical and mental distress because of an excessive or insufficient responsiveness. Such people may achieve excellence in their occupations and make valuable contributions to society. This may explain the paradox of the fine line between genius and madness. In clinical medicine, however, only morbidly dysfunctional personalities are treated.

Because personalities are affected by circumstantial events, such as a traumatic experience or psychosis arising from prison confinement, it is near impossible to understand the nature of the abnormality. It is necessary to differentiate cases of trauma from other organic cerebral diseases whenever the trauma is associated with an anatomical change in the brain. For example, it is important to differentiate traumatic pleurisy from tubercular pleurisy, and these should be differentiated from chest pain caused by a bruise. When a person suffers from an anxiety-based disorder following traumatic experience, as in some cases of *shinkeishitsu*, s/he may develop habitual headaches. In someone diagnosed with hysteria, the trauma may manifest itself as motor paralysis; whereas, in someone with an antisocial personality disorder, the trauma may induce the person to become antagonistic or aggressive. In summary, the effects of traumatic experience on a person is dependent on her or his unique disposition.

In conventional classifications of abnormal personality, classification is made and labels are assigned according to the symptoms, various characteristics of conditions, or associated historical events. Freud, for instance, who was absorbed in the search for specific events that cause neurosis, did not attend to the classification of specific kinds of illnesses. I think this lack of attention to assessment leaves something to be desired.

The terms *alcoholic poisoning* and *morphine poisoning* relate to the causes and the consequences of the poisoning. These conditions occur mainly in individuals with weak-willed dispositions and seldom in those with a *shinkeishitsu* disposition. That is, if a person abuses alcohol on one occasion or enjoys the taste of alcohol, s/he is not necessarily dependent on alcohol. Yet in some cases, one drink can be taken as an abnormal, impulsive act. I have observed a person who was dependent on alcohol, but the quantity of sake (fermented rice wine) consumed in one sitting was never more than 180 milliliters. If the condition occurs in individuals with a sensitive and weak-willed disposition, treatment becomes more effective as the inclination to *shinkeishitsu* increases and less effective as the inclination to weak-willed disposition increases. For individuals who are exclusively weak willed of the pure type, treatment and recovery are difficult.

I think that assessment and diagnosis requires a scrutiny of the client's environmental living conditions, characteristics, and the origin of her or his symptoms. Concrete facts of the client's daily life can be determined by careful inquiry, followed by an investigation of her or his past illnesses and psychological health, particularly when s/he reports symptoms of headache, insomnia, irritation, indignation, inability to work, panic attacks, or obsessive thoughts. An obsessive disorder can appear in those diagnosed with *shinkeishitsu* and compulsive acts can appear in those diagnosed with a weak-willed constitution. The early stage of delusion in schizophrenia may resemble an obsessive disorder; and transient, obsessive disorders occasionally occur in hysteria. However, no policy for treatment or prognosis can be established on the basis of diagnoses from symptoms alone.

Since about 1918, when I began to classify personalities, I thought that *shinkeishitsu* needed to be distinctly differentiated from a weak-willed character. In 1922, when I observed cases in detail, and in the light of Kretschmer's (1921) investigation, I often found it difficult to differentiate the two. For example, there are cases of intellectual impairment accompanied with *shinkeishitsu* and a weak will. In this instance, if the diagnosis is made carelessly and hastily such clients may be mistakenly diagnosed as having hebephrenia, a type of schizophrenia that occurs at puberty with restricted symptoms.

Taking actual clients from the two major types of psychosis, namely manic-depressive psychosis and schizophrenia, Kretschmer (1921) studied the relationship between temperament and somatotype. He collected the data on subjects through biographical writings and studied people with psychotic features as well as those considered healthy. He classified people by the similarity of their temperaments. He was able to publish a number of useful articles as a result of his tremendous effort. According to his studies, there are certain relationships between temperament and somatotype, and various conditions related to heredity and physical development can result in personality differences. For instance, a person whose mother has hysteria, whose father has *shinkeishitsu*, and whose grandfather has a weak will may show a mixed temperament that could result from the genetic transmission of hereditary factors that are either dominant or recessive. If, for example, one attempts to differentiate *shinkeishitsu* from hysteria, there is difficulty because temperaments overlap. Kretschmer (1921) demonstrated that the parental temperament is not always transmitted from parent to child through heredity; temperament is based on very intricate relationships across multiple factors.

I have classified personality according to psychological inclinations and have changed the conventional framework for classifying personality disorders. The nature of hysteria has been clarified to a certain extent and the somatic symptoms and complicated psychological manifestations of this disorder fall into the same category. There are many other conditions and disorders in my classification system that have never been noted by conventional investigators. Therefore, I present my criteria for assessing abnormal personality in order to obtain investigators' comments and criticisms.

Classification of Dispositions

A. Inhibition of Mental Development

　　1. Intellectual deficiency with moderate mental retardation (the mental level is at most that of a seven-year-old child);

　　2. Intellectual deficiency with mild mental retardation (the mental level is at most that of a thirteen year old);

　　3. General intellectual deficiency (the mental level is at most that of an eighteen year old).

B. Personality Structures Susceptible to Disorder
　　The following are my classification of dispositions that lead to disorder:

　　1. Hypersensitive disposition (leading to *shinkeishitsu*);

　　2. Hysteric disposition (leading to hysteria);

　　3. Weak-willed disposition;

　　4. Emotional hyperthymic (manic) disposition;

　　5. Depressive disposition;

　　6. Persistent disposition;

　　7. Other disposition;

　　8. Schizophrenic temperament.

Hypersensitive personality leading to shinkeishitsu. I have reviewed *shinkeishitsu* at length throughout this text and refer the reader to the corresponding sections.

Hysteric disposition leading to hysteria. I regard hysteria as an emotionally hypersensitive disposition. Each symptom of the abnormality is provoked by a precipitating event that triggers the predisposition. I attempt to explain all the various symptoms of hysteria in relation to emotions. A person with this disposition is extroverted in nature, lacks introspection, and cannot control her or his behaviors by intellect or logic; whereas a person with *shinkeishitsu* has impulse control. Kraepelin (1914) regarded hysteria as a type of mental underdevelopment. The emotionally hypersensitive character of hysteria is likened to a child's emotional hypersensitivity. Even though hysteria presents a specific emotional response and an ineffective way of adapting to life's circumstances, those with hysteria may have excellent intellectual ability.

When the pathology of hysteria is understood by the features of the hysteric disposition, it is not necessary to consider stigmata (a pathological term used to indicate marks on the skin, which bleed during certain mental states) as a diagnostically necessary symptom; although it has conventionally been considered the most important indicator of hysteria. In practice, many types of hysteria lack specific stigmata.

I think that the theory of the unconscious, which has been used to explain the psychopathology of hysteria, is actually apt to make the understanding of this disorder more difficult. In my view, the symptoms of *shinkeishitsu* can be explained by one's awareness, whereas those of hysteria cannot be explained in this way. In contrast to hysteria, a person with *shinkeishitsu* is often aware of the origin of the symptoms because of her or his capacity to respond from the intellect to the context. Since hysteria incites an emotional response, a person with hysteria is not aware of circumstantial events linked to the symptoms. It is this major difference that distinguishes hysteria from *shinkeishitsu*. For example, a person with *shinkeishitsu* and one with hysteria may experience fear at the sight of a person having a stroke;

that is, they share the same circumstantial events. However, the person with *shinkeishitsu* will be intellectually obsessed about attacks of fear, leading to dizziness or fainting, while the person with hysteria will show emotional reactions at each given opportunity and come to manifest hemiplegic fixed symptoms through autosuggestion.

The symptoms of hysteria that result from an hysteric disposition are divided into the following categories: (a) *hysteric temperament* wherein morbid mythomania, constitutional alteration of emotions, and so on, belong to this category; they may appear, disappear, and reappear in the person's daily life; (b) *somatic hysteria* wherein symptoms manifest in the body; and (c) *hysteric psychosis* wherein emotional outbursts, delirium, somnambulism, personality change, mania, or delusions occur.

Weak-willed disposition. Those with this condition have conventionally been called "deviant or antisocial personality." These personalities are labeled as abnormal in a very narrow sense. Such clients show a flattening of affect, demonstrate a weak-willed state, and lack the drive for self-preservation, improvement, and self-development. Those with intellectual impairment and a weak-willed constitution initiate little activity and show a lack of curiosity.

Quite often, clients with weak wills and average intellectual abilities are impulsive in behavior and get carried away with desire for immediate gain. Their behavior lacks the intellectual control that comes with self-awareness. Such individuals go heart and soul into anything they attempt, but then grow less enthusiastic over time. They often go to extremes, love the challenge of adventures, and are frequently foolhardy. Matsubara placed those with schizophrenia into this category. I think, however, that it is often difficult to differentiate schizophrenia from a weak-willed disposition when the onset of schizophrenia is characterized by a flattening of affect and a decline in will.

Emotional-hyperthymic (manic) disposition. The emotional-hyperthymic disposition is divided into three types: (1) constitutional excitability, (2) mild mania, and (3) manic state.

Although Kraepelin (1914) stated that mania and depression should be included in the same category, there are many cases that do not support this premise. Matsubara (1920) insisted that these are separate categories. A person with mania will be seized with melancholia after the mania subsides, while a person with depression will be seized with hyperthymia following an episode of depression. These changes are a reaction to the previous state. It is rare that mania and depression coexist to an equal degree or alternate with each other. I occasionally encounter cases when clients with catatonia show excitement and later find relief from it, only to fall into a stuporous condition and then find relief again. Thus, these conditions occur alternately and are apt to be misunderstood as a manic-depressive episode. Since the main condition in mania is hyperthymia, slight melancholia accompanies this condition as a natural outcome. In this sense, I think it is useful to regard mania and depression as separate categories.

It is easy to think that differences in individual temperament are linked to internal organic secretions. For example, an individual with deficient thyroid secretion will develop moderate mental retardation with flattening of affect, while an individual with hypersecretion of the gland will show excessive emotionalism as present in those with Basedow's disease (Graves' disease). Changes in the internal secretions of the parathyroid gland, gonads, and other glands seem to be related to various temperaments.

Individuals with a hyperthymic disposition are apt to suffer mild mania following various events. Some occasionally show severe mania even though they do not show a markedly hyperthymic disposition during ordinary life, just as an ordinarily gentle person may become wild after drinking. The symptoms of mania gradually intensify; they start with mild hyperthymia at the onset, reach a peak as a result of the extended rising emotion, and then repress gradually after a certain period. The phenomenon of the extended rising emotion is similar to the experience of anger that increases during thoughts of indignation. This phenomenon is like the pattern of aggravation via the *seishin-kōgo-sayō*.

Depressive disposition. This includes constitutional depression and depression.

Persistent disposition. Persistent disposition is demonstrated in (1) one's pathological inclination toward trouble making and quarreling; (2) one's religious fanaticism and dogmatic belief system; and (3) one's demonstration of paranoia.

I have insisted that paranoia exists at the foundation of many personality disorders as discussed in the medical journal *Ikai-Jiho*. Delusions in paranoia are quite different from the genuine delusions in schizophrenia with paranoia in terms of their characteristics and manner of development. I term this condition "pseudo-delusion," as it is merely a paranoia of illusions. Some cases of religious paranoia or pathological quarreling occur as a result of rigid attachment to a certain fixed outlook on life, as occurs in those with a pathologically eccentric conduct. The reader is referred to my book *Meishin to Moso* (Superstition and Delusions).

Other dispositions. Often, these dispositions lead to behaviors that are disruptive to others.
1. Simple weak-willed character
2. Impulsive disposition (exhibits reckless extravagant behaviors, and wanders without a purpose)
3. Social deviant disposition
4. Substance-abuse and substance-dependent disposition
5. Sexually deviant disposition
6. Impulsive disposition
7. Obsessive disposition
8. Compulsive disposition

The symptoms of many disorders can be explained on the basis of the weak-willed disposition. Investigators have traditionally paired obsessive disorders and compulsive disorders. I think that they differ from each other completely in terms of their characteristics. Clients with compulsive acts are difficult to treat and even if they do improve, their disorder resurfaces.

It is difficult to differentiate prison psychosis from schizophrenia and progressive paralysis because clients with mental weakness are liable to show confusion, excitement, and delirium following imprisonment; upon release, they often show schizophrenialike symptoms. Some cases of schizophrenia and general paralysis occur as a matter of course among cases of prison psychosis following the prison term. Prison psychosis is transient and can be cured because the onset is associated with confinement and the weak-willed disposition. In addition, various transient psychological abnormalities can occur in those with intellectual disabilities who have a weak-willed disposition.

Schizophrenic temperament. This was recently added to my classification following the research by Kretschmer (1921). This temperament, which has basic characteristics similar to schizophrenia, shows dissociation and a nonunity of mind with disharmony. Individuals with this temperament speak and act beyond the expectations of ordinary people and may develop schizophrenia, though some live their entire lives without suffering from schizophrenia. Some cases of eccentric conduct and impulsive psychosis may belong to this category.

references

Note: In keeping with practices of the 1920s, Morita did not publish a complete list of references in his original manuscript. This reference list was researched by the editor and includes all the sources that were part of the entire original manuscript. However, the reader is cautioned that some of these references may be incomplete or mistaken. The decision to include an exhaustive list was taken in order to assist the reader who may want to return to the original Japanese text.

American Psychiatric Association. (1994). Diagnostic and Statistical Manual (DSM-IV) (4th ed.). A.P.A., Washington D.C.

Beard, G. M. (1880). *A practical treatise on nervous exhaustion (neurasthenia): Its symptoms, nature, sequences, treatment.* New York: W. Wood and Company.

Bergson, H. (1920). *Mind-energy, lectures and essays.* W. Carr, trans. New York: Holt and Company.

Bergson, H. (1912). *An introduction to metaphysics.* New York: Putman's Sons.

Binswanger, O. (1911). *Grundzuege fuer die Behandlung des Geistes Krankheiten.* Vortrage fuer prakt. Therapie H. 3. Jena: Fisher.

Casper, J. L. (1861–1865). *A handbook of the practice of forensic medicine based upon personal experience 1861–1865* (4 vols.). London: The New Sydenham Society.

Charcot, J. M. (1877). *Lectures on the diseases of the nervous system.* London: The New Sydenham Society, 325.

Cramer, A. (1904). *A Pathologische Anatomie der Psychosen, Im Handbuch der Pathologischen Anatomie des Nerven Systems.* E. Flatau, L. Jacobsohn und L. Minor.

Cramer, L. J. (1905). *Die Nervositaet.*

DuBois, P. C. (1908). *The psychic treatment of nervous disorders: The psychoneuroses and their moral treatment.* E. Smith and W. White, eds. and trans. New York: Frank and Wagnalls.

Einstein, A. (1920). *The Einstein theory of relativity: A concise statement.* New York: Brentano.

Freud, S. (1896a). Heredity and the aetiology of neuroses. Standard Edition, 3:143–56.

———. (1896b). *The aetiology of hysteria.* Standard Edition, 3:191–221.

———. (1900). *The interpretation of dreams.* Standard Edition, 4:1338; 5:339–714.

———. (1915). *The unconscious.* Standard Edition, 14–161.

———. (1916–1917). *Introductory lectures on psychoanalysis.* Standard Edition, 15 and 16.

Hartenberg, P. (1921). *Les timides et la timidite.* F. Alcan. 192–193.

Hakuin. (1757). *Yasen-Kanna.* Kyoto.

Imamura, S. (1917). A lecture on hysteria at Asahi-Shinbun Hall on July 26, 1917.

Ishikawa, S. (1910). *Psychotherapy.* Tokyo.

James, W. (1890). *The Principles of Psychology.* New York: H Holt.

James, W. (1922). *The Emotions.* Baltimore: Williams and Watkins Co.

Jolly, F. (1877). *Hypochodorie: Handbuch der speziellen Pathologie und Therapie,* vol. 12. Leibzig.

Kraepelin, E. (1914). *Lectures on clinical psychiatry.* T. Johnstone, eds., translated from the German second edition. New York: Harcourt Brace.

Kretschmer, E. (1921). *Physique and character: An investigation of the nature of constitution and of the theory of temperament.* [Körperbau and Charakter]. Sprott, W. J., trans. New York: Harcourt Brace.

Kure, S. (1916). *Psychotherapy*. (2d ed.). Japanese Internal Medicine Compendium, vol. 2, no. 3. Tokyo.

Marui, K. (1925). *Shoniki seishin-eisei to seishinbunseki-gaku. (fu: Seishinbunseki-ryōhō, kyoiku-bunseki oyobi shoni bunseki-ho.)* (The mental health in the infantile period and psychoanalysis, with appendixes of psychoanalytic therapy, educational psychoanalysis and psychoanalytic method of children.)

Matsubara, S. (1920). "Constitutional anatomies in the neuroasthenia." *Journal of Neurology* 19, 6: 255–60.

Montessori, M. (1909). *Montessori method: Scientific pedagogy as applied to child education*. In *The Children's Houses,* Anne E. George, trans. New York: Frederick Stokes.

Shimoda, M. (1925). *Saishin seishinbyo-gaku no Jobun* (Preface of "The Latest Psychiatry"), 3d ed., Tokyo.

———. (1942). *Seishin Eisei Kōwa* (Lectures on mental hygiene). Iwanami Shiten, Tokyo.

Usa, Genyu. (1925). "Moritashi shinkeishitsu-ryōhō ni yoru chiryo seiseki." (A report of the effects of treatment of Shinkeishitsu patients by Morita's therapy.) *Journal of Neurology* 1, vol. 26.

Weygandt, W. (1905). Beitrag zur Lehre von den psychischen Epidemics cited in *General Psychopathology*, (7th ed.). Hoenig, J. and Hamilton, M., trans. (1963) Manchester University Press.

Ziehen, T. (1898). *Psychtherapie: Lehe buch der allgemeine therapie und der therapeutischen methodik*. Berlin: Herausgegeben von Eulenberg und Samuel.

———. (1908). *Psychiatrie fuer Aerzte und Studierende bearb*. von. Dr. Med. Th. Ziehen. Leibzig: S. Hirzel.

———. (1910). *Behandlung der einzelnen Formen des Irreseins*. 4 aufl. Jena.

index